D1321469

Merchant Taylors' School Library

Earth ▲ *Science*
Discovering the secrets of the earth

THE EARTH'S RESOURCES

Atlantic Europe Publishing

◆ Atlantic Europe Publishing

First published in 2000 by
Atlantic Europe Publishing Company Ltd
Copyright © 2000
Atlantic Europe Publishing Company Ltd
Reprinted 2001

All rights reserved. No part of this publication may be reproduced, stored in a retrieval system, or transmitted in any form or by any means, electronic, mechanical, photocopying, recording or otherwise, without prior permission of the Publisher.

Author
Brian Knapp, BSc, PhD

Art Director
Duncan McCrae, BSc

Editors
Mary Sanders, BSc and Gillian Gatehouse

Illustrations
David Woodroffe, Simon Tegg and Julian Baker

Designed and produced by
EARTHSCAPE EDITIONS

Reproduced in Malaysia by
Global Colour

Printed in Hong Kong by
Wing King Tong Company Ltd

Suggested cataloguing location
Knapp, Brian
  Earth Sciences set of 8 volumes
  Volume 8: *The Earth's Resources*
  1. Geology – Juvenile Literature
  2. Geography – Juvenile Literature
  550
ISBN 1 862140 68 5

Acknowledgements
The publishers would like to thank the following for their kind help and advice: *Alcan International, British Alcan Aluminium plc, The British Coal Corporation, BP International, ICI (UK), NASA, The Syndics of Cambridge University Library, The United States Geological Survey.*

Picture credits
All photographs are from the Earthscape Editions photolibrary except the following:
(c=centre t=top b=bottom l=left r=right)
courtesy of *British Alcan Aluminium plc* 33cr, 33bl; *The British Coal Corporation* 4/5, 38b, 47b; *BP International* COVER, 2b, 6b, 30b, 37b, 49cr, 49b; *ICI (UK)* 58; *NASA* 50tl; *The Stock Market* 52b; *The Syndics of Cambridge University Library* 39br, 40tl (Ernest Brown), 40cl (J. N. Macartney, The Bendigo Goldfield Registry); *USGS* 40cr.

This product is manufactured from sustainable managed forests. For every tree cut down, at least one more is planted.

Contents

Chapter 1: Wealth beyond dreams

Our lives depend on air, water, food – and rocks. We need all of these in order to live. Rocks contain the minerals that weather into soils and provide the nourishment for plants. But rocks provide us with many other things that are essential for life. There are vast amounts of useful materials hidden in even the most ordinary of rocks. Rocks provide the oil, coal, natural gas and other fuels that we use to power our world. Rocks contain minerals that give us iron and steel, aluminium and gold, copper, silver and many other metals. The metals, plastics and building materials that make up most of the goods we use, all come from the earth.

The value of the wealth in the rocks has long been understood. Wars have been fought by countries eager to gain more of the earth's riches for themselves; and hundreds of thousands of people have rushed frantically to places where gold, silver and other precious metals have been discovered.

Unlocking the wealth

Some minerals occur uncombined with other minerals, that is in their native state. But in general, much effort is needed to use the earth's riches. The fact that we now use them so widely is the result of thousands of years of experience by people experimenting with the rocks around them.

The reason why it is not obvious that the earth's rocks contain many useful things, is because they are locked up as CHEMICAL COMPOUNDS, and they need to be treated in some way before they can be used.

Iron, for example, is one of the world's most valuable minerals, but because the iron content of most iron-bearing rocks is low, to most people ironstone appears as a dull red, blue or grey rock

(Below) Coal being mined in a surface pit. Geologists have to make sure that coal seams are of good quality, and sufficiently thick, before the tremendously expensive business of mining begins.

(Above) This piece of rock contains a high percentage of iron. It is therefore an iron ore, but it is not immediately obvious that it contains iron in useful quantities.

with little obvious use. To get iron metal, the rock has to be heated at very high temperatures and processed with other chemicals (in this case limestone and coke). Then it will flow out of the rock as a liquid metal.

To make use of the earth's rocks and minerals therefore requires:

• an understanding that the earth contains a range of materials that can be useful

• a knowledge of where to look for the best deposits of the mineral required (prospecting)

(Below) Geologists use all sorts of clues to tell them about the rocks below and their potential for containing useful minerals. These are mud volcanoes in the oil-rich area of Azerbaijan.

• a knowledge of which deposits can be processed economically, and how the minerals can be extracted from the waste rock.

Prospecting is made more cost effective through a knowledge of the way in which rocks have formed in the past, and an understanding that natural geological processes can concentrate useful elements and minerals.

Thus, making use of rocks and minerals requires a knowledge of almost all the branches of earth science. It is, in fact, the business of putting geological knowledge to work for the benefit of humankind.

The place to begin is with a knowledge of the minerals that make useful resources. This is the purpose of the next chapter.

(Below) This diagram shows, in one scene, many of the locations of geological resources. Notice that the ores are found both near ancient magma chambers and in sedimentary rocks. Fuels mostly occur in sedimentary rock, but oil and gas become concentrated only in areas where the rocks are domed.

The diagram also shows how mining and quarrying take place, both on the surface and at depth.

You can also see from this diagram that some places may be easier to exploit than others. For example, it will be far harder to exploit and transport a resource from a mountain than it would from close to a navigable river.

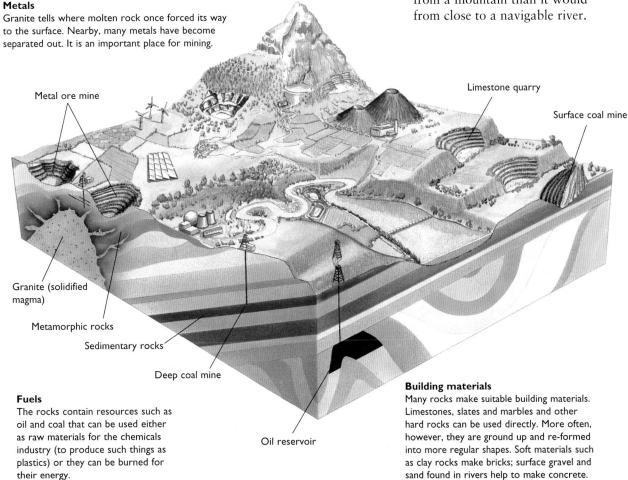

Metals
Granite tells where molten rock once forced its way to the surface. Nearby, many metals have become separated out. It is an important place for mining.

Metal ore mine

Limestone quarry

Surface coal mine

Granite (solidified magma)

Metamorphic rocks

Sedimentary rocks

Deep coal mine

Oil reservoir

Fuels
The rocks contain resources such as oil and coal that can be used either as raw materials for the chemicals industry (to produce such things as plastics) or they can be burned for their energy.

Building materials
Many rocks make suitable building materials. Limestones, slates and marbles and other hard rocks can be used directly. More often, however, they are ground up and re-formed into more regular shapes. Soft materials such as clay rocks make bricks; surface gravel and sand found in rivers help to make concrete.

Chapter 2: Ore minerals

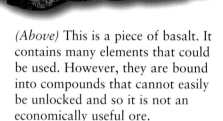

In order to understand where to find the materials we need, it is important first to identify the rocks that contain concentrations of minerals that are high enough to be useful.

An **ORE** is a piece of rock that contains sufficient of an **ELEMENT** to make it worthwhile mining and processing it.

The world's most abundant metal elements are aluminium, iron, magnesium, manganese, and titanium. All other metals, for example, copper, lead, zinc, gold, and silver, are scarce, even though some are in everyday use.

However, just because a mineral is abundant, it does not mean that it is easy to extract it from the rocks in which it occurs. For example, basalt, which is made up of the minerals olivine and hornblende (which are compounds containing magnesium and iron) and feldspar (which is a compound containing calcium and aluminium), have these elements all locked up in compounds that are not easy to separate. Thus, although basalt is the world's most abundant

(Above) This is a piece of basalt. It contains many elements that could be used. However, they are bound into compounds that cannot easily be unlocked and so it is not an economically useful ore.

(Below) Just because a mineral is a small percentage of a rock, it does not make it worthless. In some cases it is easy to extract and is so valuable that it is worth mining entire mountains away for it. This is the case for the element molybdenum. This picture shows the Climax molybdenum mine in Colorado, USA. The whole shape of the mountain has been changed by mining.

rock, it is not mined for its minerals at all because the metal elements are extremely difficult (and expensive) to extract.

Another example is ilmenite (which is an iron-titanium oxide). It contains the metallic elements magnesium, iron, calcium, aluminium and titanium, but the metals are such tiny proportions of each mineral that it is not worth trying to extract them.

From these examples, you can see that many rocks are not suitable for use as sources of elements. Only those rocks which have undergone some special natural geological process that enriches the rock, will be suitable. This is why it is very important to be clear which ores are economically useful.

Types of ores

Ores can be found in IGNEOUS, METAMORPHIC and SEDIMENTARY rocks. The amount of element in an ore does not need to be high if the element is very valuable. Gold, platinum and other metal elements may occur as only a few grammes of metal per tonne of rock, but remain valuable ores.

About 40 metal-containing ores are commonly mined. The most easily smelted or refined metals are referred to as the ORE MINERALS. However, the ore minerals are nearly always found intermixed with minerals that have no value. These are called GANGUE. The valuable mineral <u>and</u> the gangue (which normally comprises the majority of the rock) make up the ore.

Ore minerals are grouped by their chemical compounds. The main groups are: native metals, sulphides, oxides and hydroxides, and carbonates. You may notice that the silicate group is missing from this list. This is because, although silicates are the most common minerals in the world, they are not used as ore minerals because the cost of extracting the metals from them is prohibitively high.

(Below) This is a sample of dolomite (white crystals) and iron pyrite (yellow cubic crystals). The ore is pyrite (iron sulphide) and the gangue is the dolomite.

(Below) This is a typical sample of an ore. The conditions that allow the formation of pyrite are also right for the formation of crystals of other compounds (which together make up the material called gangue). Separating the desired minerals from the gangue is often a very complicated chemical process.

Native metals

Some elements can be found on their own and uncombined with other elements because they are not very reactive. These are known as the native metals. The important ones include copper, gold, platinum and silver.

Native metals can be found as VEINS, narrow cracks filled with minerals, that cut through other rocks. Because they require no processing to separate them from other elements, native metals are easy to use.

Gold and platinum are principally found as native metals. Several other native metals – silver, copper, and iron, for example – rarely occur in large enough deposits for them to be important sources of the metals today. However, ancient civilisations used native metals extensively because they did not have the means to work with metal ores.

To be useful, native metals have to occur in large pieces, and this is not at all common. Nevertheless, when they do occur like this, they often give prospectors spectacular wealth and cause a rush of speculators to try their hand at mining.

(Above) Native silver.

(Below) Chalcopyrite (iron and copper sulphide).

Sulphides

The most important compound to produce useful ores is the one formed when a metal occurs in combination with sulphur. This compound is called a sulphide. Copper, lead, zinc, nickel, molybdenum, arsenic, antimony, bismuth, cobalt, gold, silver, platinum and mercury all form sulphide ores.

In many deposits, all or most of these metals occur together, so that the mining of one or more

major metals also allows the recovery of others as by-products. Thus, for example, cadmium and indium are produced almost entirely as by-products of zinc sulphide smelting.

Oxides

Another group of common compounds that produce useful ores is the oxides – a metal in combination with oxygen. Aluminium, chromium, iron, manganese, tin, titanium and uranium are mainly found in the form of oxides.

Carbonates and silicates

A third common ore is a combination of a metal with carbon and oxygen. This makes a compound called a carbonate. Although carbonate minerals are common – iron, manganese, and magnesium are all found as carbonates – they are the least preferred ore bodies from which to extract metals because extraction is much more expensive from carbonates than from sulphides and oxides.

Silicates are not used at all because the cost of extraction is too high.

(Above and below)
Haematite, iron oxide.

Common metal ores

Aluminium

The main source of aluminium in the world is bauxite. This ore forms in places where the aluminium compounds become especially concentrated. Bauxite is a tropical clay with a high proportion of aluminium oxide. It is a secondary mineral and forms only microscopic crystals. It is colourless or greyish-white. It is formed in the same places as iron oxide and the bauxite ore is, therefore, stained with red iron oxide.

Modern bauxite mines are located where at least half the volume of the ore is aluminium oxide. All of the ores are soil layers and thus they are always mined in shallow open-cast pits. Today, the majority of bauxite comes from Guinea, Australia, Jamaica and Brazil.

Bauxite – Hydrated aluminium oxide (gibbsite $Al(OH)_3$)
Colour: White, but often associated with iron oxides and, therefore, appears orange.
Hardness: 2
Cleavage: None
Crystals: None. Massive but normally found as granules (called pisoliths)
Streak: White
Other: Specific gravity 4

Bauxite rock has an orange-red colour because of staining by iron oxides.

Chromium

Chromium is a hard, steel-grey metal that takes a high polish, and is used in alloys to increase strength and corrosion resistance. Stainless steels are alloys of chromium and iron.

Most of the compounds of chromium are highly coloured, and the colours of emerald, serpentine, and ruby are all due to chromium.

Chromium occurs as chromite – an ore of iron and chromium.

Chromite – Iron chromium oxide $FeCr_2O_4$
Colour: Black
Hardness: 5
Cleavage: None
Crystals: Cubic
Streak: Dark brown
Other: Specific gravity 4.3–5.0; it is weakly magnetic. It is formed in many basic igneous rocks.

Chromium minerals are often brightly coloured when refined.

Green chromite.

Copper

Copper occurs in a number of forms. Because it is not a very reactive element, it sometimes occurs uncombined (as a reddish-bronze native metal). The shape reflects the deep underground fissures in which it was originally deposited and is known as a dendritic pattern. The largest piece of native copper ever found was in Minesota Mine, Michigan, USA. It weighed over 500 tonnes.

Copper is more commonly found as an oxide, a sulphide, a carbonate and a silicate. Each of the compounds tends to have a characteristic colour, allowing it to be identified in the field. Copper silicate and copper carbonate have a characteristic green colour.

A piece of native copper

Malachite – Copper carbonate $Cu_2CO_3(OH)_2$
Colour: Green
Hardness: 4
Cleavage: Perfect in one direction, fracture conchoidal
Crystals: Monoclinic
Streak: Green
Other: Specific gravity 4; often shows concentric colour banding; rare as crystals but usually as nodules.

A secondary copper mineral that develops in hydrothermal deposits as they are altered over time. Often found with azurite.

This is banded malachite, a copper carbonate and a useful ore.

Chrysocolla – Copper silicate $Cu_2H_2Si_2O_5(OH)_4$
Colour: Greenish-blue
Hardness: 4
Cleavage: Brittle and glassy, fracture conchoidal
Crystals: Monoclinic
Streak: White
Other: Specific gravity 4; often found in massive pieces. It occurs with malachite and limonite.

A fist-sized piece of chrysocolla ore.

(Above) Copper extraction at the Morenci Mine in Arizona, USA.

Chalcopyrite – Copper iron sulphide $CuFeS_2$

Colour: Brassy yellow that tarnishes to deep blue

Hardness: 4

Cleavage: Poor

Crystals: Tetragonal

Streak: Greenish black

Other: Specific gravity 4, slightly above average; brittle mineral. Another mineral (along with pyrite) that is sometimes mistaken for gold.

One of the main ores of copper; often found in the same deposits as bornite and pyrite. Chalcopyrite is very widely found in metamorphic rocks, especially in schists. Chalcopyrite and bornite (see below) together provide half of the world's copper metal.

A nodule containing chalcopyrite.

Bornite – Copper iron sulphide Cu_5FeS_4

Colour: Copper-red when fresh, but usually seen as the tarnished form, which is deep blue, hence the name of the ore is peacock ore.

Hardness: 3

Cleavage: None

Crystals: Cubic

Streak: Grey-black

Other: Specific gravity 5, a moderately heavy mineral.

It occurs in several environments, for example, with calcite in carbonates, with galena in metamorphic rocks and with quartz in veins close to magma chambers.

A piece of bornite or peacock ore with speckles of chalcopyrite.

Gold

An unreactive metal found entirely as a native metal, either as veins or as PLACER DEPOSITS.

Native Gold – Gold Au

Colour: Gold-yellow

Streak: Gold-yellow

Hardness: 3

Cleavage: None

Crystals: Cubic

Other: Specific gravity 15–19 (very heavy)

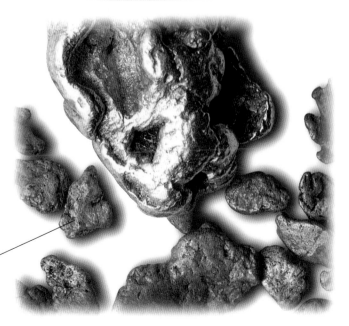

Native gold. The flakes in this picture are each about 3 mm long.

Iron

Iron is the second most abundant metal (after aluminium) in the earth's crust. It is a reactive element and is rarely found as a native metal; most commonly bound into compounds containing oxygen called iron oxides. Most iron ore is haematite and magnetite (sometimes containing over two-thirds of their weight as iron).

Magnetite – Iron oxide Fe_3O_4
Colour: Black
Hardness: 6
Cleavage: None
Crystals: Cubic
Streak: Black
Other: Specific gravity 5; it is magnetic. It is formed in many igneous rocks. It is also found in sedimentary rocks.

Magnetite, or lodestone, is normally found as a brown or black mass in igneous and metamorphic rocks as well as in some veins. Magnetite is often found associated with chromite, an oxide of chromium.

Magnetite covered with iron filings to demonstrate its magnetic properties.

Haematite – Iron oxide Fe_2O_3.
Colour: Steel-grey on fresh face and reddish-brown when tarnished
Hardness: 6
Cleavage: None, fracture splintery
Crystals: Hexagonal
Streak: Red
Other: Specific gravity 5; slightly above average; brittle mineral.

It has a very high iron content, often over two-thirds of the ore. One of the main ores of iron and is found in igneous, metamorphic, and sedimentary rocks. Varieties include kidney ore.

Haematite.

Pyrite – Iron sulphide FeS_2
Colour: Pale or brassy yellow (hence fool's gold)
Hardness: 6
Cleavage: None
Crystals: Cubic with **STRIATIONS** on the faces
Streak: Greenish black
Other: Specific gravity 5; pyrite produces sparks when struck against a steel penknife blade. Is sometimes mistaken for gold. Often found in the same deposits as bornite.

Also known as 'fool's gold'. Pure pyrite contains 47% iron and 53% sulphur.

Iron sulphide is not used primarily as a metal ore, because its high sulphur content is difficult to remove. But, it is mined to produce sulphuric acid, and it is regarded as a gangue mineral when copper or zinc ores are being mined.

Cubic crystals of pyrite. Parallel 'scratches', known as striations, are a common feature of pyrite crystals. The colour may range from a pale gold to brassy.

Lead

Lead is widespread, occurring in the same location as other metals such as gold, silver and zinc. Most concentrated metal deposits are formed in hydrothermal veins.

Lead mines are sometimes found in areas of limestone or dolomite that once had magma chambers below them. Limestones have many natural fissures through which hot minerals can easily flow.

Lead sulphides have dark grey, cubic crystals, and leave a grey streak of colour. Galena is the main source of lead for the world's industries.

Lead is most commonly seen as crystals of lead sulphide (PbS), where it is known as the mineral galena. It also occurs as cerussite (lead carbonate, $PbCO_3$) and anglesite (lead sulphate, $PbSO_4$). Lead minerals tend to be very heavy, about three times as dense as most rocks.

Galena – Lead sulphide PbS
Colour: Dark lead-grey. Does not tarnish
Hardness: 3
Cleavage: Perfect three directions
Crystals: Cubic
Streak: Dark grey
Other: Specific gravity 7.5, a heavy mineral.

Lead sulphide has some of the features of a metal, being bright and shiny, but others of a non-metal; like salt, it is brittle.

The cubic structure and dull grey colour of lead sulphide shows very clearly in this specimen.

Manganese

Manganese is mainly found as an oxide, for example pyrolusite, or as a carbonate, for example, rhodochrosite. These ores are only worked when they contain more than 35% manganese, and are mainly mined in Australia, Brazil, Gabon, India, South Africa, Ukraine, and Georgia.

Pyrolusite – Manganese dioxide MnO_2
Colour: Black
Hardness: 5
Cleavage: Perfect in one direction
Crystals: Tetragonal, usually as massive columns
Streak: Sooty black
Other: Specific gravity 4.4–5.0, slightly above average; powdery black mineral

One of the main ores of manganese; found in hydrothermal veins.

Molybdenum

This is a silver-grey metal used to add strength to steel. It is a relatively rare element.

Molybdenite – Molybdenum sulphide MoS_2
Colour: Bluish lead-grey
Hardness: 1
Cleavage: Perfect into sheets
Crystals: Hexagonal
Streak: Grey-black
Other: Specific gravity 5, a moderately heavy mineral; feels greasy; can be confused with graphite, but graphite is blacker. Occurs as thin sheets (scales).

This mineral is found with quartz, cassiterite and chalcopyrite. Molybdenite is the most important ore of molybdenum.

Nickel

A silvery-white metal that resists corrosion.
It does not occur in native form, however.
Its most common form is as niccolite,
a compound of nickel with arsenic.

The most important sources are
pentlandite, pyrrhotite and millerite and
chalcopyrite. All of these are sulphides.
They occur with chalcopyrhite.

Nickel

Platinum

Platinum is one of the group of elements
called heavy metals.

Platinum – Native platinum Pt
Colour: Tin-white to grey. Does not tarnish
Hardness: 4
Cleavage: None
Crystals: Cubic
Streak: Light grey
Other: Specific gravity 14–19, a very heavy metal.

Platinum is formed in deep-seated, intrusive,
igneous rocks, but it is rarely found in this form.
Equally rare are nuggets, or any other substantial
piece of metal. Nonetheless, this does not mean
that platinum is rare. In fact, it is very widely
distributed around the world, mostly in placer
deposits.

Tin

Tin is important because it is a very poorly reactive
metal and so can be used to protect other metals
from corrosion.

Cassiterite – Tin oxide SnO_2. One of the main ores
of tin; found in hydrothermal veins.
Colour: Brown to black
Hardness: 6
Cleavage: Distinct
Crystals: Tetragonal, usually as twinned crystals
Streak: Light brown
Other: Specific gravity 7; heavy mineral. The most
common tin-bearing mineral.

Cassiterite

Zinc

The most abundant and important zinc minerals are zinc sulphide (sphalerite or zinc blende) and zinc carbonate (smithsonite). Zinc sulphide is the most common of the two, occurring as dark crystals. Zinc is found among many other metals in hydrothermal replacement deposits.

Sphalerite – Zinc sulphide ZnS
Colour: Yellow, red-brown or green and looks resinous
Hardness: 4
Cleavage: Perfect six directions
Crystals: Cubic
Streak: Light brown
Other: Specific gravity 14–19, a very heavy mineral.

Pure sphalerite is colourless, the colours being given to the mineral by iron impurities. Red to yellow-coloured sphalerite does not look like a metal, being transparent or translucent and looking something like dull amber. Black sphalerite looks more metallic. Sphalerite containing cadmium is bright orange.

Zinc sulphide is the most abundant and important zinc mineral. It is also called zinc blende.

The resinous red-brown crystals on the ore sample are sphalerite.

Encrustations of blue-green zinc carbonate.

Smithsonite – Zinc carbonate (ZnCO$_3$)
Colour: White to green
Hardness: 4
Cleavage: Perfect in three directions to form rhombohedrons
Crystals: Hexagonal
Streak: White
Other: Specific gravity 4.3–4.5

Found most commonly in limestone areas in veins that also contain lead. Zinc carbonate probably originated as a hot solution of zinc sulphide which was precipitated on reacting with the calcium carbonate (limestone).

Chapter 3: Where ore minerals are found

How is it that minerals sometimes become concentrated as native metals, sulphides, oxides and carbonates when elements are normally widely dispersed in the rocks of the earth's crust? If they can answer this question, it will help geologists find ores more efficiently.

In practice, ores can be found in all kinds of rock, igneous, metamorphic and sedimentary. However, the processes at work in each environment are very different.

Minerals that form in magma chambers

Magma chambers (also the sources of volcanoes) are large bodies of molten rock that form within the earth's crust. The upper parts of the magma may have up to several per cent of water dissolved in them.

When the magma chamber ceases to become active and begins to cool, the molten magma begins to solidify by creating crystals.

During crystallisation, the first minerals to form are those that do not incorporate much water, for example, feldspar. As they use up mineral matter but no water, the water content of the remaining magma increases, making the magma more runny. Material in a more runny magma can now flow more easily, enabling growing crystals to scavenge suitable atoms over a wider area. In this way they are able to grow very large. Rocks containing large crystals are called PEGMATITES. Pegmatites are an important source of many rare metals, sheets of mica and some gemstones.

(Below) Many very pure ores form near to masses of molten rock. As fingers of molten rock force their way through cracks, they heat up water in the surrounding rocks, making it very acidic. Most metals dissolve in extremely hot acidic water, so that, as the water filters through the rock and cools, the minerals come out of solution one at a time, forming veins. This is the reason why gold, silver, copper, tin and lead can often be found at various levels in a single mine. This is a gold-bearing vein in an Australian gold mine. A large piece of gold found in an ore is called a nugget.

Other concentrations of metals occur in igneous rocks, called carbonatites. These rocks are rich in calcium and form huge deposits, with high concentrations of rare metals, even though they contain no large crystals.

In magmas low in silica, the magma is, in any case, quite runny, and minerals can separate out in the melt (this is called SEGREGATION). As a result, some parts of the magma may contain pockets of just one mineral. The chromite mined in the Bushveld Complex, South Africa, is an example of this. Vanadium is another metal that separates out in this way; again, mostly mined in South Africa.

Sometimes, cooling magma will produce a liquid, which is saturated in a particular mineral. When this happens, part of the mineral will precipitate out. If this is a metal compound, it can lead to highly concentrated ores being formed inside the magma. Iron sulphide (pyrite) is the most common mineral formed in this way. As it precipitates, the iron sulphide scavenges other metals, such as copper, nickel and platinum. The world's largest platinum mine, the Merensky Reef of the Bushveld Complex, South Africa, exploits one of these deposits. The Kambalda nickel deposit in Western Australia is actually a precipitate that formed in a lava.

The Precambrian-aged Sudbury Igneous Complex in Ontario, Canada, is an ore body in an igneous rock

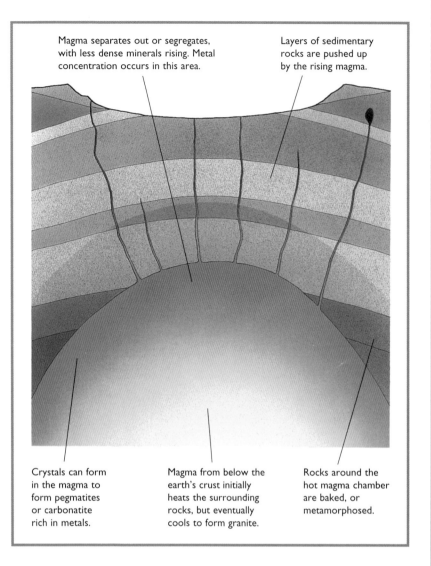

Magma separates out or segregates, with less dense minerals rising. Metal concentration occurs in this area.

Layers of sedimentary rocks are pushed up by the rising magma.

Crystals can form in the magma to form pegmatites or carbonatite rich in metals.

Magma from below the earth's crust initially heats the surrounding rocks, but eventually cools to form granite.

Rocks around the hot magma chamber are baked, or metamorphosed.

(Above) At the top of a magma chamber, hot fluids push their way into cracks and fissures in the overlying rocks. Here, the liquids cool, and the minerals solidify as crystals. These places, called hydrothermal veins, are where miners look for a wide range of highly prized minerals including metals and precious stones.

60 kilometres long by 28 kilometres wide and is shaped like a funnel pointing into the rock. Layers of this funnel are rich in copper, nickel and platinum sulphides. The melting of this rock may, unusually, not have been melting from magma coming from below, but melting caused by the collision of a meteorite with the earth. The magnetic iron ores called magnetite may also have been formed as precipitates from cooling magmas or lava. The huge iron ore deposits at Kiruna in northern Sweden are of this kind.

(Above) Kiruna iron ore mine, Sweden. The mine exploits an ore shaped like a vertical lens. The mine has removed all of the centre of the mountain and the actively mined area is far underground.

Minerals that form close to magma chambers

While some concentration of metals occurs inside the magma, and so is found within granites and other igneous rocks, much more is formed by very hot watery liquids that eventually boil off from the magma, and push their way into the surrounding fractured rock.

You can imagine this hot liquid as probably being something like hot brine (hot salty water). This liquid is able to dissolve rock. At the same time it can transport NATIVE METALS as well as compounds.

The water for this purpose may be ejected from the magma or it may seep through the fractured rock from the ground surface and be heated as it reaches the magma. Half the weight of a solution of this kind can be made of dissolved minerals.

CASE STUDY: Silver in America

Silver attracted Spanish colonists into the Americas in the 17th and 18th centuries, and the discovery of the Comstock Lode in Nevada in the 19th century caused a silver rush.

The Comstock Lode was a rich deposit of silver discovered in Nevada. It was named after Henry Comstock, part-owner of the property where it was discovered in June 1859. The resulting silver rush caused the rapid growth of many silver towns including Virginia City and Washo.

So much silver was found in the lode that a United States branch mint was opened in nearby Carson City. The richness of the lode was used as a way of persuading the United States to admit Nevada to the Union.

In the peak years of 1876–78 silver ore worth about $36 million on average was mined each year. But the lode was finally exhausted about a decade later. Virginia City became a ghost town.

These watery solutions (called HYDROTHERMAL FLUIDS) are common. Most of the time the solutions escape to the surface and leave no trace; only in special conditions, such as when the solutions fill cracks that are closed at one end, or fill a porous rock, do they start to deposit minerals.

There are two reasons why minerals begin to form. Sometimes the solutions cool and solidify. Or the solutions react with minerals in the surrounding rocks, causing some of the minerals to precipitate out.

(Below) This diagram shows some of the mineral-forming environments associated with igneous activity.

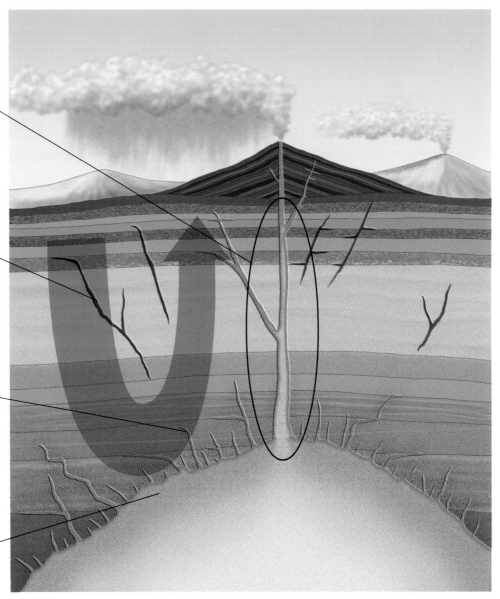

Porphyritic ore bodies occur in veins surrounding vents. Here, the country rock is extensively shattered. Former vents that led from magma chambers to volcanoes can contain high mineral concentrations.

Gases boiling off the magma may condense in cracks away from the magma chamber to create rich ore bodies.

Watery magma will force its way into the shattered rock surrounding the magma chamber. It will cool and solidify in narrow cracks to make veins. Patterns of veins are called **LODES**.

The addition of water in the upper zone of the magma chamber, makes the magma more runny and able to flow into the surrounding shattered rock.

Veins and lodes

Closed spaces filled with minerals that have formed from hydrothermal solutions are called veins by geologists, and important veins are known as lodes by miners.

Famous lodes started gold and silver rushes and were found at Comstock in Nevada and Cripple Creek in Colorado, USA.

Important sources of metals include the tin-copper-lead-zinc lodes of Cornwall, England; the gold-quartz lodes of Kalgoorlie, Western Australia, and Kirkland Lake, Ontario, Canada; the tin-silver lodes of Llallagua and Potosí, Bolivia; and the silver-nickel-uranium lodes of the Erzgebirge, Germany.

Some veins have a mixture of large and small crystals. These are called PORPHYRITIC. If they have concentrations of metals, for example, copper, they are called porphyry-copper deposits.

(Below) Copper mining in Arizona includes areas that are copper porphyries. Many are worked by open-cast methods, leading to the opening out of huge pits.

(Below) This diagram shows where minerals can be found in a landscape after the mountains have been partly removed by erosion.

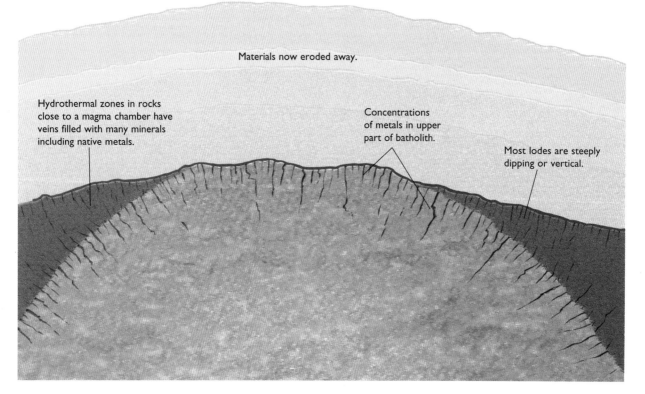

Materials now eroded away.

Hydrothermal zones in rocks close to a magma chamber have veins filled with many minerals including native metals.

Concentrations of metals in upper part of batholith.

Most lodes are steeply dipping or vertical.

Typically, porphyries are found as a large volume of shattered rocks, criss-crossed with huge numbers of small veins. What has happened is that the shattering has made the rock very permeable, so that hot fluids could simply and easily work their way through it and then crystallise.

About half of all copper in the world is mined from this kind of deposit. Molybdenum is another common mineral found in such shattered rocks.

The proportion of rock to mineral is large in all of these deposits, with perhaps 1 part copper mineral to 99 parts rock. Nevertheless, such deposits are very profitable if they can be mined from the surface. One of the world's biggest molybdenum mines, the Climax Mine near Leadville, Colorado, USA, is of this kind. The only way to mine it has been to take the mountain apart.

When hydrothermal fluids invade limestone or marble, the acid waters react with the limestone and precipitate minerals. Veins in limestone and marble are called SKARNS. Magnetite iron, copper, zinc, tungsten, and molybdenum are commonly found in skarns. One of the most famous skarns was discovered at Cornwall, Pennsylvania, USA. It was first worked in 1737 and provided iron ore for two and a half centuries. Tungsten skarns are an important source of this metal. One of the largest mines is King Island, Tasmania, Australia.

Pine Point in the Northwest Territories of Canada is a famous lead and zinc sulphide skarn deposit. In the past, similar deposits in the Yorkshire Dales and in Cumbria, England, gave rise to widespread early lead and zinc mining.

Large deposits of similar origin are found at Broken Hill in New South Wales, Mount Isa in Queensland, and McArthur River in the Northern Territory, all in Australia. In these cases the minerals are deposited in ash, rather than in limestone.

(*Above*) Many 'caves' prove to be mines opened out by miners exploiting skarns in limestone districts, but now abandoned. This is a long-abandoned lead mine in England.

CASE STUDY: Broken Hill, New South Wales, Australia

Broken Hill (named after the shape of the nearby hills) lies northeast of Adelaide. It is called Silver City because of the enormity of the mineral deposits of silver, lead and zinc that are found in the rocks there.

Mining began in 1833 and the Broken Hill Proprietary Company, Ltd (BHP), was formed in 1885 and has now become Australia's largest company.

Broken Hill grew rapidly because of the availability of work. Most of Australia's lead exports come from this location. The ore is mined at Broken Hill, concentrated by milling, and then sent by rail to Port Pirie in South Australia for refining. Zinc is also mined. Both ores are sulphides and the sulphur is extracted and used in the manufacture of sulphuric acid.

Minerals in volcanoes

When volcanoes erupt under the oceans, seawater can react with the volcanic rocks. This is another way of producing a hydrothermal solution and, thus, of concentrating the metals as sulphides. Hot springs can be seen depositing minerals on land and on the ocean floors today, just as they have throughout most of geological time. Deposits of this kind are rich in copper, lead and zinc. The world's most famous places for mining this kind of deposit are in Japan. Known as Kuroko deposits, they may contain about a fifth of metal by weight. The ancient mines operated by the Romans in Cyprus (from which the word copper comes) are also of this kind.

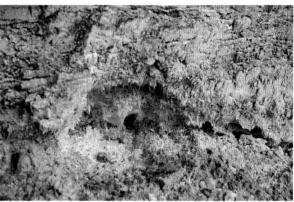

(Above) Sulphur being deposited from the waters rising from hot springs, New Zealand.

Minerals from ancient lakes and coasts

Ores can be found in some sedimentary deposits, although most prove to be very ancient (**PRECAMBRIAN** times) when conditions in the oceans were very different from today. Sedimentary iron ore of Precambrian age is one of the world's largest mineral resources. It produces banded iron formations, which consist of bands of iron mineral separated by bands of sand.

(Below) Changes in temperature and chemical content cause waters flowing from hot springs to precipitate many minerals. Although the ones surrounding these hot pools do not contain useful minerals, you can see the principle clearly.

One of the largest banded iron ore deposits is found near Lake Superior in the United States. The thin sheets of ironstone stretch for hundreds of kilometres, and represent material precipitated on the floor of an ancient shallow sea. The Hamersley Basin in Australia has a similar deposit.

Many of these are very ancient deposits, often 2 billion years old, and were probably formed in environments quite different from those of today. At that time there was much less free oxygen, and so much more iron remained dissolved in the oceans. The source of the iron was probably underwater volcanic eruptions. Precipitation of the iron began

when plants developed and began to release oxygen. As soon as oxygen became freely available, the soluble iron reacted with it and formed insoluble oxides, which then precipitated out of the water.

Another kind of iron ore was formed much more recently, commonly in JURASSIC times. At this time in the history of the earth, sand grains rolling about on coasts, seem to have acted as centres for iron to deposit. Most of the Jurassic ironstone deposits of Europe are of this kind, for example those in French Lorraine and in the English Midlands. Their presence is partly responsible for the location of the first industrial cities in the Industrial Revolution. Similar rocks in North America are called the Clinton Formation.

Minerals are also deposited whenever lakes or seas dry out. The dissolved minerals form layers on the dried-out bed and their build up year after year creates thick beds of salt, soda ash, borax and other minerals. All of these are called EVAPORITE DEPOSITS, and they can form beds many tens of metres thick.

(Below) Evaporite deposits forming on the floor of a desert. From time to time this is a lake. Evaporites also form in coastal lagoons. This is Bristol Lake, California, USA.

Ancient salt beds are mined worldwide, including those in Cheshire, England, and in Poland. In Poland, the mines are so large that a cathedral has been built inside one of the mine caverns.

Coal from ancient swamps

Coal is a metamorphic rock, meaning that the plants from which it is made have been changed due to heat and pressure through long periods of burial. Metamorphism in organic material works at far lower temperatures and pressures than are needed for metamorphism in inorganic rocks. As a result, coal is found interbedded with sedimentary rocks and it is not found with other metamorphic rocks.

The degree of metamorphism determines the grade or purity of the coals – how much carbon it contains.

Coal begins as thick beds of poorly decaying plant material in swamps and bogs. The first stage of decomposition creates peat, but this is not thought of as a form of coal because no alteration has taken place.

A number of stages follow that turn the peat into a rock. First, the plant matter must be covered over by a layer of sediment to prevent air getting to it and oxidising the peat to carbon dioxide gas. This only occurs if the land sinks or if the sea level rises while the swamp is still actively accumulating material. The overlying sediment gradually consolidates to a rock. Because of its weight, and the weight of subsequent layers of sediment, the process of transformation begins. To make rock, compression from the overlying sediments has to reduce the water content from the 75% it is in peat, to a small percentage in the final rock.

The lowest RANK of material that can be called coal, that is the softest coal, still brown in colour and with a high enough water content to still be soft, is known as brown coal or lignite.

The process of metamorphism is much more

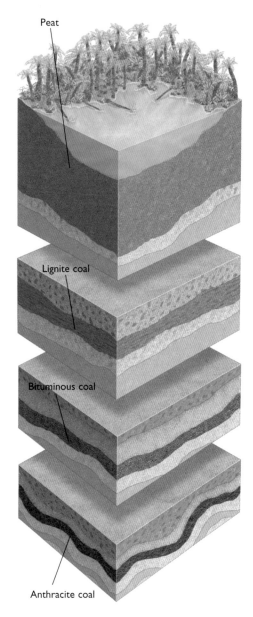

Peat

Lignite coal

Bituminous coal

Anthracite coal

(Above) A diagram of the relationship between the various types of coal. As the coal is buried more deeply, its carbon content increases, and the thickness of the seam decreases. The original peat contains about 50% carbon, lignite coal contains 70% carbon, bituminous coal contains 85% carbon, and anthracite coal contains over 90% carbon.

complete in the first of the hard coals, known as bituminous coal. This is medium rank coal. The driest coal, with the highest carbon content and the greatest degree of metamorphism, is the high ranking coal known as anthracite.

The most widely found type of coal is bituminous. It can be used as a source of fuel and as a raw material for making a range of chemicals by distillation. Anthracite is used as a domestic (smokeless) fuel, while lignite is used only to fuel large power stations.

Coal has not formed uniformly throughout geological time. In the earliest periods of geological history there were no plants, and then most of the early plants were marine. Only when plants became adapted to the land was it possible for swamps to form.

However, the presence of land plants is not sufficient for coal formation. Extensive swamps tend only to grow in the tropics, because the conditions there are right for rapid growth and thus for the accumulation of large amounts of plant matter.

Furthermore, there must be extensive areas of shallow sea that, from time to time, rise up to become land and then sink again. In this way, very large areas

(Above) Bituminous coal.

(Above) Cyprus swamps in Louisiana, USA, give a feel for the kind of place where the plants for coal lived in the past.

(Left) Coal is concentrated into seams among sedimentary strata. A part of a seam is shown being blasted out in this picture.

of swamps can be formed that can be engulfed by the sea and covered by deposits of sand or mud that eventually form rock.

The **CARBONIFEROUS PERIOD** was the first time when all of these conditions were met (although there are some local deposits of coals from earlier periods, some of which must have been formed under the sea from algae, none of them is commercially useful).

Petroleum from sea bed sediments

The word petroleum comes from the Latin word *petra* and *oleum*, meaning 'rock oil'. It relates to all the substances that are found in sedimentary rocks as either liquids or solid, and which originate from the decomposing bodies of microscopic sea life. Petroleum therefore includes oil, as well as natural gas. Most petroleum deposits occur as a mixture of both liquids and gases.

Petroleum is a mixture of hydrocarbons (the chemicals that make up the liquids and gases are all combinations of the elements hydrogen and carbon) and smaller amounts of other elements such as nitrogen, oxygen, sulphur, and some metals.

(Below) Test drilling to determine the geology at a location.

Petroleum products are not just fuels, but also raw material for making plastics, paints, fibres, fertilisers and so on.

Unlike coals, where the deposition of plants happened with no further decay, in the case of the bodies of microscopic organisms, decay is a major factor. The burial of the organisms provided another important ingredient for petroleum formation, because the chemical reactions that occur during decay depend on temperature. Deep burial resulted in the temperature rising to about 100°C. Some liquid

hydrocarbons are produced at temperatures as low as 65°C. All liquid hydrocarbons are destroyed as temperatures rise above 175°C, although gases survive high temperatures.

As the decomposition continues, so liquids and gases are produced. What happens next depends on the texture and structure of the host rock.

Petroleum is less dense than water and does not mix with it. In the early stages of petroleum formation it may exist as tiny globules in the water in rock pores (much as fatty globules exist in a washing-up bowl of soapy water).

As the rocks begin to compress more, they expel some of their water upwards. Thus, the compaction of the rocks may force out water and, with it, the globules of oil and bubbles of gas. Eventually, the globules come together to make bubbles of petroleum large enough to begin to become buoyed upwards through the denser water, and at this stage a petroleum field starts to form.

(Above) Crude oil.

Petroleum reservoirs and traps

Most petroleum is found in pools. These are called PETROLEUM FIELDS (or just oil fields and natural gas fields if only one kind of product occurs).

Some petroleum pools can stretch over tens of kilometres and be hundreds of metres deep. Others can be quite small.

The fact that petroleum is found in pools, means that it must have flowed from where it was produced and become concentrated into the pools. This can only happen in a PERMEABLE ROCK where the pores are connected together. A permeable rock, such as sandstone or limestone, which hosts petroleum, is called a RESERVOIR ROCK.

An impermeable rock, such as a shale, cannot

(Above) A nodding donkey extracting oil from a shallow oil field in Texas. The pressure in the rock is almost enough to recover the petroleum and only small pumps are needed.

develop petroleum fields (although it can be rich in dispersed petroleum as in the important oil shale rocks).

In a region where rocks slope, oil and gas can rise through the water and displace the water downwards. The best structures for this to happen in are domes and tilted rocks that are closed by faults (see diagrams). Tilted rocks that also change texture can also be traps. Thus, if a sandstone changes to a mudstone and the rock is tilted with the mudstone part of it higher than the sandstone part, it will stop any further rise of the petroleum. These structures are called traps. SALT DOMES provide yet more traps.

If the permeable rock has a connection to the surface, light oil and natural gas will move upwards and escape. Surface seepages can be large enough to give workable deposits of tar, or asphalt. The presence of active seeps in an area gives a hint that more reserves may be located underground.

Large areas of oil and natural gas occur only in places where the rocks remain covered with an impermeable cap rock.

(Below) Structures in which petroleum is found. The natural gas (white areas) is shown on top of the crude oil (brown areas).

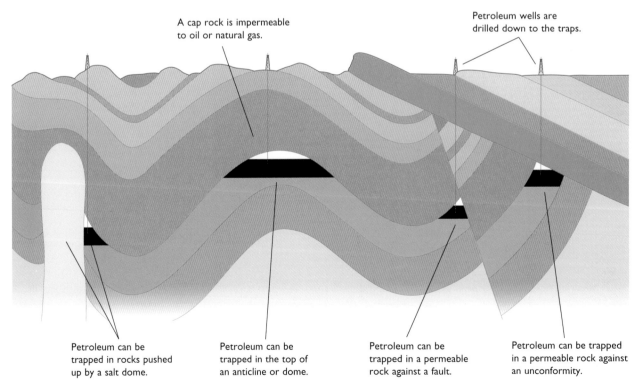

A cap rock is impermeable to oil or natural gas.

Petroleum wells are drilled down to the traps.

Petroleum can be trapped in rocks pushed up by a salt dome.

Petroleum can be trapped in the top of an anticline or dome.

Petroleum can be trapped in a permeable rock against a fault.

Petroleum can be trapped in a permeable rock against an unconformity.

Minerals in weathered soils

In the tropics, soils are much thicker than in the mid-latitudes. A combination of high temperatures and heavy rainfall makes rocks decompose, releasing the minerals they contain. Nearly all of the materials in a soil are dissolved away. Only the iron and aluminium oxides remain and become very concentrated. When exposed to the surface, these iron-rich rocks dry out to form a hard rock-like crust called LATERITE. These special materials are important sources of both iron and aluminium. Soils mined for their aluminium content are called BAUXITE. Nearly all of the world's aluminium comes from bauxite deposits.

Minerals of rivers and coasts

Not all minerals are concentrated as they are formed. Some become concentrated after they have weathered and are being carried by rivers or coastal waves and currents. These are called PLACER DEPOSITS.

Placer deposits are created by running water or by the action of coastal waves. If a vein, or

(Above and left) Bauxite is found in thick surface deposits. This example is in Jamaica.

other type of concentrated mineral ore, is exposed at the surface, weathering will break it up into pieces small enough to be carried by moving water.

In some cases, water will also take the mineral into solution and it will be lost. For example, sulphide minerals react with air or water containing dissolved oxygen. But, some minerals, such as the oxides of tin and magnetite iron, and native metals such as gold and tin, as well as diamond and ruby, are very resistant to reaction with water. They are also very hard and resist being worn down as they are tumbled about in the water. If these materials are also much more dense than the other material being carried by the currents, then they will tend to settle out, and in this way be concentrated.

Placer deposits are very important, and much prospecting has been done on them. More than half of all the gold mined in the world has come from placer deposits. The biggest in the world are the South African Witwatersrand gold fields. These are fossil placer deposits and are more than two billion years old. Very important tin placers are found off the coasts of Malaysia and Thailand.

(Below) Concentration of minerals due to weathering and slope transport.

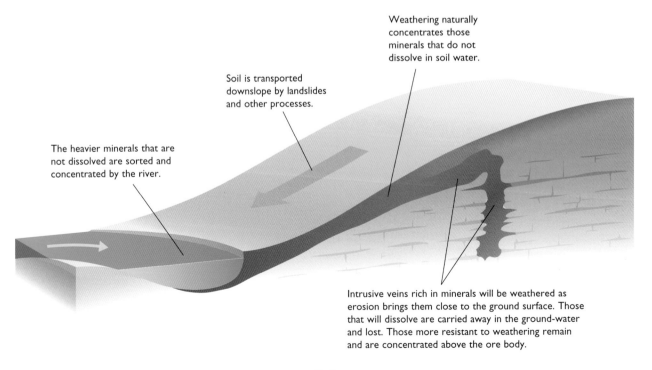

Weathering naturally concentrates those minerals that do not dissolve in soil water.

Soil is transported downslope by landslides and other processes.

The heavier minerals that are not dissolved are sorted and concentrated by the river.

Intrusive veins rich in minerals will be weathered as erosion brings them close to the ground surface. Those that will dissolve are carried away in the ground-water and lost. Those more resistant to weathering remain and are concentrated above the ore body.

Sorting by the river along its course concentrates heavier metals in the floodplain alluvium.

Wave action sorts heavy metals in nearshore deposits.

(Above) Concentration of heavy metals in river and coastal alluvium.

Location and age of minerals

The earth's resources have not formed uniformly through time, nor evenly over the surface. Rather, they have become concentrated into special parts of the world and they were formed more at certain times than at others.

Metal ores

Metal ores are not found everywhere in the world, but only in some special places. This is because the concentration of ores only occurs next to igneous rocks (that is plate margins), in the cores of mountains (where plates have collided), or in some basins where sediments are being deposited. Thus, the pattern of volcanic activity and mountain building influences the world's pattern of deposits.

Deposits are also concentrated into specific periods of the earth's history. For example, between 2.8 and 2.65 billion years ago, volcanism was especially active and large amounts of metal sulphide deposits were produced. Between 2.5 and 1.8 billion years ago, huge amounts of iron (which had previously been in solution in seawater) were precipitated on the sea bed.

Coalfields

Most coal was formed during the Lower Carboniferous Period. Coal of this age is found in the Appalachian Mountains and the interior basins of North America, in Nova Scotia, in Great Britain, Belgium, the Netherlands, France, Germany, and in Silesia and the Donetz field of southern Russia.

Coal is also found dating from the PERMIAN

PERIOD. The Kuznetsk Basin in central Siberia and the Fushun Basin in China and Manchuria have large deposits of coal from the Permian. The coalfields in Australia, India, and southern Africa are also mainly of Permian age. Permian-age coal is also found in Antarctica, although it is not mined here because of treaties forbidding the exploitation of this wilderness continent. TRIASSIC coal is much less common, being found only in North Carolina and Virginia in the United States.

The coal deposits of Jurassic age are found only in the Angara Basin in Siberia.

Coal fields from the CRETACEOUS PERIOD are important for providing the high grade coal in the western United States such as in Colorado and Wyoming.

Coal is also found dating from the TERTIARY PERIOD. This coal is found in Spitzbergen, Norway, but it also includes most of the low sulphur coal that makes the near surface coal fields of the western United States. Thick lignite beds of this age also are found near Cologne in Germany and in Victoria, Australia.

(Below) The distribution of brown coal, or lignite, bituminous (black) coal and petroleum (oil and natural gas) deposits.

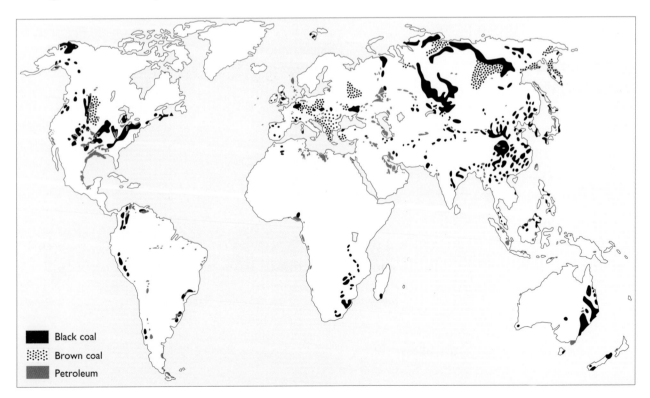

Black coal
Brown coal
Petroleum

Petroleum fields

Petroleum can form only in rocks younger than the time when marine organisms were common. Nevertheless, because simple marine organisms were already around over 3 billion years ago, the range of possible rocks is large (and much larger than for coal). However, some geological periods provide better conditions than others. The most productive periods appear to have been **ORDOVICIAN** (oldest), **DEVONIAN**, Carboniferous, Permian, Cretaceous and Tertiary.

Petroleum fields tend to occur as a small number of very large deposits known as giants. As far as is presently known, the 300 largest petroleum fields contain about three-quarters of the world's discovered reserves. It is clear that there are very many more small deposits, but they are too small to be worked profitably at this time.

Most petroleum is found not only in rocks of a certain age but also in certain parts of the world. The main petroleum fields are in the Persian Gulf, North and West Africa, the North Sea, the continental shelf of the Atlantic, Alaska, and the Gulf of Mexico. The Middle East contains two-thirds of currently known petroleum reserves.

(Below) An offshore oil rig exploiting the Permain oil deposits of the North Sea.

Chapter 4: Mining

Finding a mineral deposit is only the first part of successful use of the resource. To be profitable, the deposit must be big enough to be mined for many years, it must be easy to work, and it must be close to a means of transport (rail or ship being the cheapest).

Mineral deposits are most valuable if they are a compact shape, and not fragmented by FAULTING. If the mineral is too far from good transport, it may make even a rich, compact, unfaulted deposit too expensive to be worth mining.

Even if the deposit is rich and close to the surface, it may still be unprofitable to mine if the value of it is low. Metals tend to fluctuate widely in value and so an ore that can be worth mining at one time, may become uneconomic a few years later due to a collapse of world prices. Tin, and now even gold, are examples of this fluctuation.

(Below) In the past, coal mining was done by hand. Notice the pit props and the truck that was filled using shovels. The coal seam being mined is less than a metre thick, forcing miners to work on their knees.

The history of mining

The history of mining goes back at least 40,000 years, when ancient peoples used hard rocks called flints to make hand axes and arrowheads, and coloured (ironstone) rock as a kind of paint for their cave drawings.

The first metals to be used were those that had been loosened from the rocks in which they were formed. Most of these were found in small pieces among the sand and gravel of river beds. Gold and copper were first found in this way.

Many pure metals are heavier than stone, and they can be separated from the river bed by panning. Panning is the oldest form of mining in history.

Occasionally, people discovered veins of native metal. These were the most valuable of all resources. However, in this case, the metal had to be extracted from the rock using hand picks. If the rock was very hard, this could prove an almost impossible task.

In the Middle Ages, the arrival of gunpowder from China played an important part in mining techniques, making it much easier to extract minerals from the solid rock. Holes were drilled in the rock, filled with explosives, and then ignited. The same technique, using more sophisticated chemical explosives, is still used today.

As miners followed the pattern of natural deposits, they excavated complexes of deep vertical SHAFTS and long tunnels (ADITS or GALLERIES). The shafts had to be made safe, and the miners had to find ways of getting the mined material to the surface. Small railways were first developed in mines, although much material was moved by hand or using animals.

Collecting ores was almost always done by underground mining methods, even when the deposit was quite close to the surface. The reason for this is that, in the days of hand mining, there simply wasn't any way to remove the surface materials (called OVERBURDEN).

In the West Midlands of England, for example,

Panning

The accumulation of gold in river sediments is known as a placer deposit. The gold can be separated out by hand in a method known as gold panning. Because it is heavy, gold resists being washed away. The gold particles can be separated from sand by swirling the pan around in a little water. The gold will remain in the centre of the pan while the sand swirls off the edges.

The sluice box is a much more efficient way of collecting gold. The larger pebbles are screened away and the other fragments washed down a chute. Bars placed along the chute collect the heavy gold, while the rest is washed away. Washing river sediment over wool fleeces is another way to collect gold.

Most placer deposits, especially those worked in navigable rivers and in coastal areas, are now mined on a far larger scale using dredgers. Thousands of tonnes of sediment a day may be washed by a single machine. Four-fifths of the world's tin is obtained from placer deposits.

(Above) One development in panning was sluicing, where the sediment was placed on a frame through which water continuously ran. Baffles down the chutes retained the heavy metals.

Early mining was not a large-scale affair, but was run by many independent owners. As a result, the amount of money put in to the mine was small. This picture shows a 19th-century mine in Edmonton, Canada.

Gold rushes

Because people have put such a high value on gold, its presence has attracted much attention throughout the ages. One of the main reasons for Spanish and Portuguese explorers taking an interest in South America was to plunder them as a source of gold.

The 19th century saw several major gold rushes in the United States, Canada, Russia, South Africa and Australia. The 1848–49 gold rush in California produced more new gold than had been found in the previous three centuries and made the United States the largest gold producer in the world. But, as these gold fields were worked out, others took their place in Alaska, Australia (particularly Victoria) and South Africa (the Transvaal). Of the probable gold reserves, about half are to be found in the Witwatersrand area of South Africa.

Mining depended on large amounts of labour to do everything from mine the resource to tow away the waste rock or fix pit props. When many people worked on neighbouring claims, the result was near chaos.

By the 1920s mines had become much more mechanised. Trains could carry away ores and bring in supplies or fuels. Shafts, pumps and crushing plants were run by machines, often driven by electricity, not steam. Mining had almost entered the modern age.

which was the cradle of the Industrial Revolution, coal seams lie quite close to the surface. Nevertheless, people dug mines that were just a few metres deep. Many of them were known as bell pits because of their shape. The early industrial landscape was dotted with such bell pits. Once machines were developed that could remove large amounts of overburden, mostly underground mining became mostly surface mining. This change only happened in the last half of the 20th century.

Modern surface mining

Surface mining costs much less than underground mining. As a result, over two-thirds of the world's mineral production now comes from surface mines.

Strip, hill and valley and open pit mining are all kinds of surface mining.

Strip mining

Strip mining is a system used when level beds of mineral lie just below the surface over a large area.

Strip mining opens up large areas of ground, and in the past caused widespread scarring of the landscape when land was simply left after use. Today, land is reclaimed after use. Strip mines are often open for about five years before they are filled in and another site opened up.

The modern, conservation-oriented technique is as follows. A long trench (a strip of land) is dug down to the mineral level. The overlying waste rock and soil, the overburden, is stripped away and put to one side for return when the site is reclaimed after mining.

The mineral is dug out and the trench widened. The waste from this extension is placed in the worked out part of the trench, so that, as mining progresses, the trench is refilled. As a result, only a limited amount of overburden has to be placed on the land surface. When the site is worked out, the final strip is filled in with the overburden extracted from the first strip, and the topsoil replaced.

Surface coal and bauxite are mined this way. Strip mining now also accounts for about two-thirds of coal extraction.

(Below) Strip mining.

Exposed ores or coal is removed and carried away in dumper trucks or on conveyor belts.

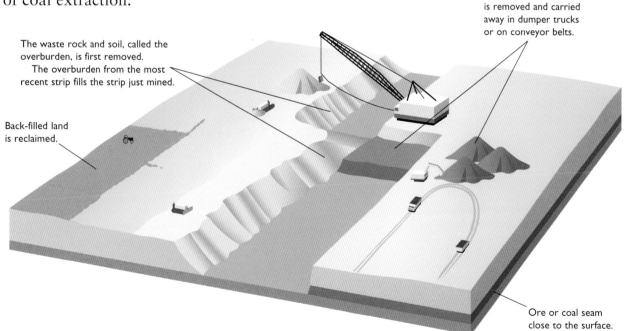

The waste rock and soil, called the overburden, is first removed.
The overburden from the most recent strip fills the strip just mined.

Back-filled land is reclaimed.

Ore or coal seam close to the surface.

Hill and valley mining

Where the land is hilly, the mineral may have to be extracted across the valley side, following the contour. In this case, the whole top of a hill may be removed gradually and the fill placed in nearby valleys. This can have the benefit of making the reclaimed land flatter and easier to use in later years for farming and other purposes.

Open pit mining

Where the mineral is at shallow depth, and especially when it is of a compact shape, mining may proceed by digging an open pit. This open pit is never filled in and so remains as an eyesore in the landscape.

The pit is dug to leave a series of terraces – called benches – about 15 metres high and a spiral ramp for the trucks that have to remove the overburden and mineral.

The pit is enlarged by blasting back into each bench. The ore is drilled and then blasted so that excavators can carry it away. The use of explosives on the surface requires far less skill than when they

(Below) Benches around the sides of a disused open-pit copper mine.

are used underground, and much larger amounts of material can be blasted clear with each firing.

The scale of the machines that carry away the blasted ore is staggering. A single scoop can contain 50 cubic metres of material weighing more than 100 tonnes. The dumper trucks used to transport the ore can each be the size of a house, and each is capable of carrying more than 100 tonnes. Much of the recovery of mineral is done with a drag-line shovel. It is possible to remove half a million tonnes of material a day by this method in the world's biggest surface mines.

The pit has to slope inwards at an angle to ensure that the rock remains stable. It is unsafe to dig a large cliff-sided pit in weak materials.

Open pit mining is very similar to stone quarrying. These mines are often therefore worked by construction companies.

(Above) A modern open-cast gold mine near Bendigo, Australia.

(Above and right) Open-cast mining operates by blasting out layers and then carrying away the broken ore.

Stone quarrying

Quarrying is designed to collect stone for building, cement making, and the like, and also sand and gravel for use in making concrete and other building materials.

Stone quarrying is still carried on widely. The most useful stones are granite, limestone, sandstone, marble, slate, gneiss, and serpentine. Most of these stones are used for building purposes, but limestone is used as a road stone and also as a raw material for cement. Salt is also quarried by underground room-and-pillar methods (see page 47).

Most quarries are on the surface, although some quarries continue underground using room-and-pillar techniques.

Unlike open pits, the quarry is normally designed to take special advantage of the natural stone, and so benches vary with the block size of the stone. Stone quarries can only make use of about a fifth of the stone quarried, the rest is unsuited to building purposes. If the stone is hard (such as gneiss or limestone), the waste can be crushed and used as road stone. Unlike the open pit, where blasting is used to shatter the rock for easy transport, building stones have to cut away from the quarry face with as little damage as possible. Most block cutting is done with a wire saw. Alternatively, a series of closely spaced holes is drilled, and the blocks are then prised away from the quarry wall, often by hammering in wedges.

(Below) Portland limestone, a Jurassic limestone with very few bedding places.

Underground mining

Underground mining uses either a horizontal tunnel, if there is access through a valley side, a sloping tunnel, or a vertical shaft. A sloping tunnel is preferred because it allows a conveyor belt to carry material directly to the surface. However, sloping tunnels can be used only when the material is at relatively shallow depths.

Underground mining has to follow the ore vein or coal seam. In the past, very thin seams were worked by hand, but machinery cannot be used on seams or veins that are less than a metre thick.

Following a seam or a vein underground can be difficult if the rock is faulted. This does not matter very much in surface mining, but frequent changes of seam height can make an underground resource unworkable.

Mining for lode tin

This diagram shows how hot fluids rising up from molten magma injected themselves into the rock surrounding the magma.

To recover this ore, deep shafts were sunk, following the near vertical directions of the deposits. The veins were typically very narrow, perhaps no more than a metre wide, something like sheets of material. The network of shafts and horizontal tunnels (adits) developed in a mine was designed to reach these mineral sheets from a number of places.

Lode ore contains a variety of impurities, including tungsten, sulphur and arsenic, most of which can be removed by a stage of roasting before final smelting. Roasting arsenic-containing ores was a hazardous process.

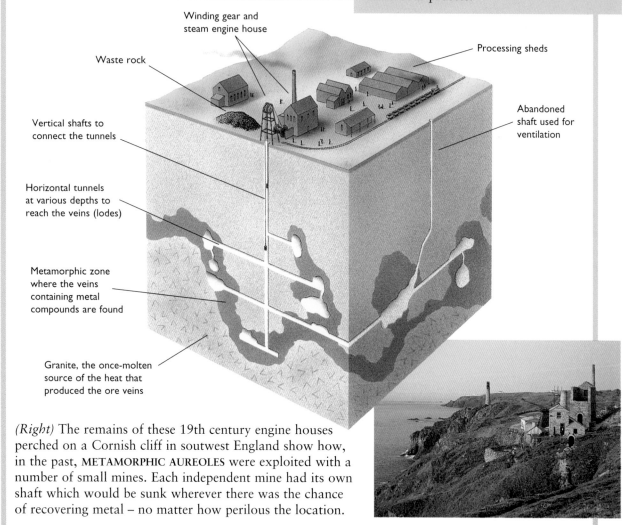

Winding gear and steam engine house

Waste rock

Processing sheds

Vertical shafts to connect the tunnels

Abandoned shaft used for ventilation

Horizontal tunnels at various depths to reach the veins (lodes)

Metamorphic zone where the veins containing metal compounds are found

Granite, the once-molten source of the heat that produced the ore veins

(Right) The remains of these 19th century engine houses perched on a Cornish cliff in soutwest England show how, in the past, METAMORPHIC AUREOLES were exploited with a number of small mines. Each independent mine had its own shaft which would be sunk wherever there was the chance of recovering metal – no matter how perilous the location.

Most mines have an access shaft which is sunk from the surface down to the many levels that may be worked. Each of the horizontal levels is connected to the shaft by a tunnel called a DRIFT. The shaft contains a winched cage for carrying both workers and ore between the mine levels and the surface. The shafts also carry pipes to pump in air, carry electricity and pump out water.

With underground mining, recovery of the ore or coal is so difficult that as little waste as possible is carried to the surface. Most miners try to leave waste rock underground.

The working face is extended by cutting or blasting. As this is done, part of the rock is removed. If removal continued, the unsupported rock would collapse. It is, therefore, vital that a way is found of supporting the roof of the mine. The most common way is called room-and-pillar. In this

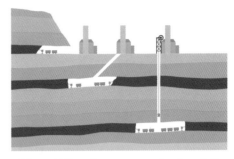

(Above) The three types of mine; left – adit; centre – sloping tunnel; right – vertical shaft.

(Below left) A deep mine is a complex of many shafts and horizontal tunnels (drifts) that are extended further and further in search of ore or coal. Problems that have to be overcome include providing ventilation for the miners, transporting ore and waste rock out of the mine, and keeping the mine dry.

Ventilation is achieved by sinking more than one shaft and by using pumps. An old system was to set a fire below a ventilation shaft so that hot air rose up this shaft and pulled cool, fresh air down the main shaft. Ventilation, drainage and transportation are now all achieved by machines.

(Below) An abandoned adit. To imagine how it worked, compare it with the diagram on the left.

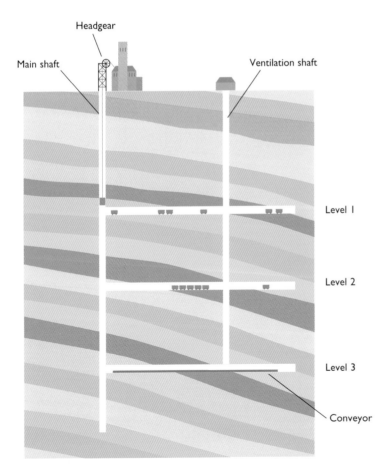

Headgear

Main shaft

Ventilation shaft

Level 1

Level 2

Level 3

Conveyor

case a pattern of pillars is left unmined as the face is extended. With soft rocks, such as salt and coal, long-wall mining is used. In this case a long wall is established for mining, using an access tunnel at each end. The wall is then mined and the roof supported by jacks. As the long wall is mined out, so the jacks are also moved, allowing the roof behind to collapse in a controlled way.

When the rocks are hard, as with the diamond and gold fields of South Africa, then mining has to be done with pneumatic drills and blasting.

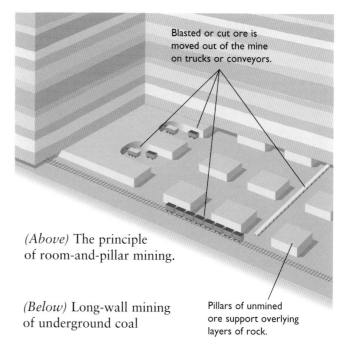

Blasted or cut ore is moved out of the mine on trucks or conveyors.

(Above) The principle of room-and-pillar mining.

(Below) Long-wall mining of underground coal

Pillars of unmined ore support overlying layers of rock.

Petroleum drilling

The discovery and exploitation of petroleum products use a unique combination of geological skills. The first stage is a survey to map the geological formations and the structures. This is done with seismic surveys, measuring the reflection of explosive-generated sound waves from the underlying rock strata. Surveyors are looking for likely traps. Satellite surveys are also used to detect minute seepages because surface seepages may indicate underground reserves.

Once a survey detects likely structures, exploration wells are sunk. Drilling produces cores, which can be examined to find the age of the rocks, and the fossils in them can give an indication of the environment in which they were formed. Experience has shown that some fossils can be used as indicators of petroleum deposits.

Once the presence of petroleum has been detected, a trial well has to be sunk. Wells are drilled by using a steel bit attached to a drill pipe, which revolves and cuts its way downwards. At the same time, mud is pumped down to keep out water and prevent any sudden rush of petroleum if a field is located.

When the drill reaches petroleum-bearing formations, a casing pipe is lowered into the hole and a valve put on top of the pipe to control the flow of petroleum. The surface valve is called a 'Christmas tree'.

One successful well does not establish the size of the field and so more test drillings have to be made. Production begins when it is clear that there are substantial reserves.

A single well cannot extract all of the reserves from a petroleum field. This is because the rate of movement of petroleum through the reservoir rock is slow. As exploration of the field continues, production normally slows down as natural pressure on the petroleum gets lower. Most fields will

(Below) A portable oil rig drill. This is best suited to small wells (nodding donkeys) in oil fields close to the surface.

yield only one-quarter to one-third of their oil through pumping, depending on the permeability of the rock and the stickiness of the petroleum. If stickiness (viscosity) is the problem, steam may be blown into the well to raise the temperature of the petroleum and make it more runny. To flush the last reserves of petroleum, water or gas (for example, carbon dioxide) is pumped down some of the wells in order to force more petroleum from others.

When a field contains both liquids and gases, these must be separated by special equipment. The liquids are then processed in a refinery to extract the products that are needed for the fuels, plastics and other industries.

Petroleum reserves can be located kilometres below the surface and require very deep shafts. *(Above)* connecting two sections of sheathing during drilling. *(Left)* Part of a stack of pipes designed as sheathing for the well as it is sunk.

Petroleum is a bulky and relatively low value product and so it is important that transport costs are kept as low as possible. On land, oil and natural gas are collected from tanks near small well-heads by truck; larger wells are directly connected to a pipeline. Underwater (known as offshore) drilling and transport are more complicated, but very important because about a third of the world's reserves are offshore.

If possible, offshore drilling platforms are used which extend down to the sea bed. In deeper waters, floating platforms have to be used; they are anchored above the sea bed and connected to the well head by flexible pipes. Both tankers and sea-bed pipelines are used to transport the petroleum to the shore, where it can be connected to the land-based pipeline network.

Natural gas is very expensive to ship, and most natural gasfields are connected directly to pipelines. Where this is not possible, the gas is usually cooled sufficiently to turn it into a liquid before it is pumped into special ships.

The petroleum industry is actually the most recent of the fuel-based industries. The first well to be drilled dates back only to 1859. This was at Titusville, Pennsylvania, USA.

Although there are certainly more petroleum fields to be discovered in the future, exploration will have to concentrate on using rocks that are not thought of as worthwhile today. For example, some sandstones contain very thick oil. They are known as tar sands. Many shales also contain oil. These are called shale oils. The extraction of these products, however, will, for the first time, give the petroleum industry the huge problem of dealing with a vast amount of waste rock.

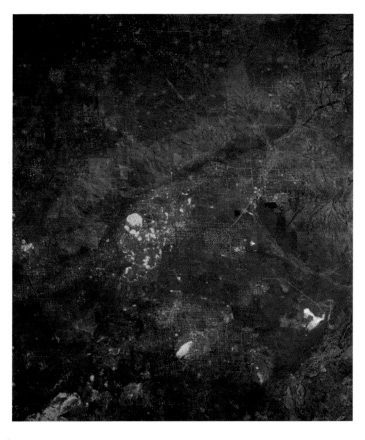

(Above) This satellite picture shows a part of Texas. You can see roads running across the area. The numerous small white blotches are places where pumps are working. This gives a clear indication of the density of wells often needed to recover oil from an oil field.

Mining by using melting points

Some materials are soluble, or can be recovered as an emulsion (a mixture of water and tiny particles of material). The main technique used to recover sulphur from buried deposits of native sulphur, for example, relies on the fact that sulphur has a low melting point, but is insoluble.

Superheated water (raised to a temperature of about 165°C) is pumped underground through a pipe. This melts the sulphur. But since the sulphur is insoluble it remains chemically uncombined. Inside the main pipe are two smaller pipes. Compressed air is pumped down a central pipe, and a frothy mixture of liquid sulphur, water and air is pushed up through the remaining pipe. This system is called the Frasch process, named after its inventor Herman Frasch, an American chemist who invented it in 1891.

Brine solution mining

Salt, potash and trona (sodium carbonate) are all soluble and so can be removed in solution.

A well is sunk to the salt bed. The well is lined (cased) and pipes inserted into the well. Water is then injected into the well through one part of the tube system. The brine is more dense than the fresh water and sinks to the bottom. The brine is then sucked up through another part of the tube system. Caverns created by solution this way can be 100 metres across. It is common to place a number of wells across the site of the mineral in much the same way as when extracting oil.

When the brine reaches the surface, the water is evaporated away using special vacuum flasks.

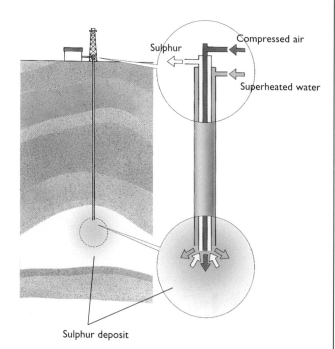

(Below) Extraction of sulphur using superheated water to melt the sulphur so that it can be forced to the surface.

Sulphur

Compressed air

Superheated water

Sulphur deposit

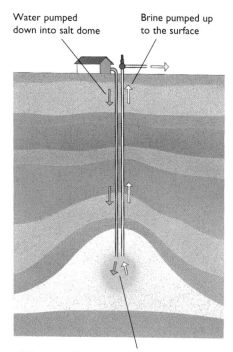

(Below) Extracting salt as a brine solution. The salt may occur as beds or as salt domes.

Water pumped down into salt dome

Brine pumped up to the surface

Water dissolves rock salt in a salt dome to make a concentrated salt solution called brine. This can then be drawn back up to the surface.

Chapter 5: Processing and refining

Once the ore, coal or crude oil has been found and extracted from the ground, it still has to be processed to make it useful. Because an enormous amount of waste material is often released during the processing, it is important for processing to be undertaken near to the mine. If this cannot be done, the cost of transport may make the mining unprofitable.

Processing an ore

Ores are a very good example of raw materials with a huge volume of waste in them. Even when a rich ore is mined, two or even three stages of concentration and purification are often still needed. First, the ore has to be crushed or ground down and as much waste rock (gangue) removed as possible. Only then is it worthwhile trying to separate the metal from its

(Below) The ore-processing complex at Mount Isa, Australia.

compound using a chemical process. These chemical processes are called roasting (which chemically changes the mineral to make it easier to react in the next stages), smelting (which produces metal with some impurities) and refining (which removes the last of the impurities).

All minerals can be smelted, but some require enormous amounts of energy to do the job. For example, because of the large amounts of energy required to smelt aluminium, it used to be one of the most expensive of metals, and it was prized along with gold and silver. It was only after the construction of hydroelectric power stations that electricity became cheaper and the cost of smelting went down, making the metal much more attractive for use in everyday objects.

In general, the amount of energy required to smelt the 95% of the earth's crust that is made of silicate minerals, makes the process uneconomic. Because it takes less energy to smelt sulphide, oxide, carbonate and hydroxide minerals, these are the main ores processed today. Silicates are almost never refined.

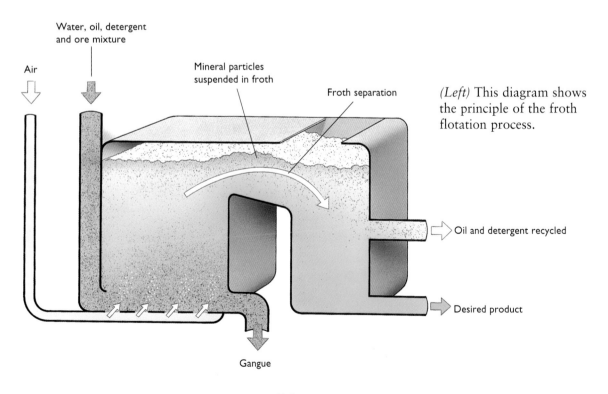

(Left) This diagram shows the principle of the froth flotation process.

Crushing

Once the minerals have been located and extracted from the ground, many further stages are needed to turn the ore into a useful metal. The first of these steps is to crush the ore into a powder. Particles in powder form are much more readily separated than when they are in large lumps.

Crushing is done in crushing and grinding mills. Once the powder has left the grinding mill, the process of concentration begins. This is done by making use of the properties of the metal ores involved. For example, iron can be removed from the gangue by using high power magnets.

Many metals are more dense than the gangue, and so techniques have been developed to separate them using flowing water, allowing the gangue to be washed off.

Flotation

The powder is placed in a vat with water, and wetting and frothing chemicals. Jets of air are blown into the vat, causing the frothing agents to make bubbles. The chemicals in the vat prevent the metals from becoming wetted by the water. Because they remain dry, they can be caught up by air bubbles and lifted to the surface of the vat, where they can be floated off and collected. The wet particles of non-metalliferous rock, by contrast, sink to the bottom (see diagram on page 53).

Chemical processing

Once the ore has been concentrated by crushing and flotation, the final stages of complete separation – roasting, smelting and refining – can begin. These are chemical processes, as opposed to the previous stages which were mechanical.

Roasting

Most naturally occurring metal ores are a complicated mixture of compounds, and it is often sensible to convert some of the compounds into a kind that are easier to smelt. Smelting works best with compounds

Smelting iron ore

The furnace has to remove the oxygen from the metal ore (the ore must be reduced), and the waste rock must be separated from the valuable metal. This is done with a very hot blast of carbon monoxide gas. The whole furnace is built so that hot carbon monoxide gas is continuously produced and blown through melting rock. The heavy slag and molten iron escape from the bottom of the furnace, and a charge of new ore and fuel is added at the top. In this way the blast furnace can be operated continuously.

The charge becomes hotter as it moves down, until it melts in the lowest region of the furnace.

The iron produced in this way is called pig iron. It is the foundation material for other kinds of iron and steel. It is rarely used without further chemical treatment because it is hard and brittle.

(Above) A modern integrated iron and steel works. The raw materials lying on the dockside in front of the furnace are introduced to the top of the furnace by a conveyor system.

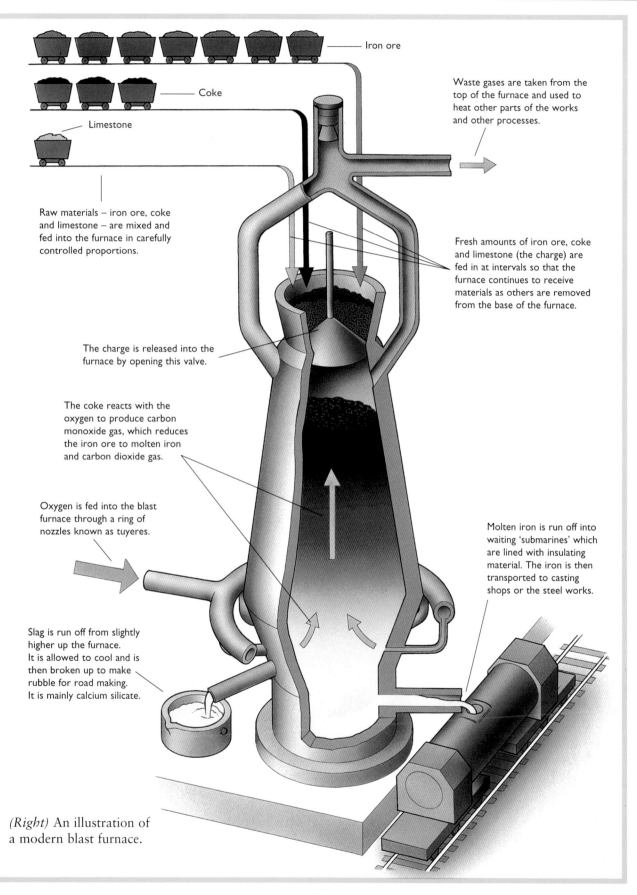

Iron ore

Coke

Limestone

Raw materials – iron ore, coke and limestone – are mixed and fed into the furnace in carefully controlled proportions.

Waste gases are taken from the top of the furnace and used to heat other parts of the works and other processes.

Fresh amounts of iron ore, coke and limestone (the charge) are fed in at intervals so that the furnace continues to receive materials as others are removed from the base of the furnace.

The charge is released into the furnace by opening this valve.

The coke reacts with the oxygen to produce carbon monoxide gas, which reduces the iron ore to molten iron and carbon dioxide gas.

Oxygen is fed into the blast furnace through a ring of nozzles known as tuyeres.

Molten iron is run off into waiting 'submarines' which are lined with insulating material. The iron is then transported to casting shops or the steel works.

Slag is run off from slightly higher up the furnace. It is allowed to cool and is then broken up to make rubble for road making. It is mainly calcium silicate.

(Right) An illustration of a modern blast furnace.

that contain oxygen. Thus if the mineral is a sulphide (which contains no oxygen), it is first converted to a sulphate (containing both sulphur and oxygen), usually by the simple process of roasting it in air. The roasting causes the sulphide to react with oxygen from the air at just below the melting point of the mineral.

Smelting

Smelting involves heating the ore above its melting point. When the ore melts, two layers form, one containing the metal and a small amount of impurity, the other containing everything else (called the SLAG).

The most commonly smelted metal is iron, the smelting taking place in a tall oven called a blast furnace (see page 55).

Some other metals are treated slightly differently. For example, some liquid metal ores can be heated sufficiently to cause the metal to become a vapour.

Example of processing a metal oxide ore by vaporising

Zinc oxide is smelted with a supply of coke and lead oxide in a furnace. The coke, being almost pure carbon, reduces the oxide to metal and produces carbon monoxide gas. The zinc metal, which has a low boiling point, forms a vapour in the smelter, and this is distilled and collected before making it into ingots.

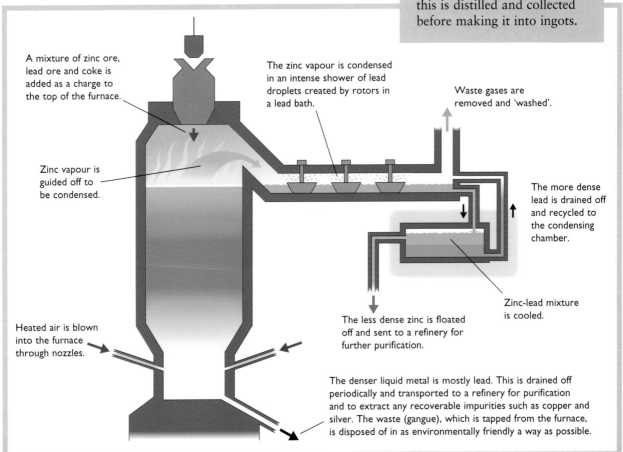

A mixture of zinc ore, lead ore and coke is added as a charge to the top of the furnace.

The zinc vapour is condensed in an intense shower of lead droplets created by rotors in a lead bath.

Waste gases are removed and 'washed'.

Zinc vapour is guided off to be condensed.

The more dense lead is drained off and recycled to the condensing chamber.

Zinc-lead mixture is cooled.

Heated air is blown into the furnace through nozzles.

The less dense zinc is floated off and sent to a refinery for further purification.

The denser liquid metal is mostly lead. This is drained off periodically and transported to a refinery for purification and to extract any recoverable impurities such as copper and silver. The waste (gangue), which is tapped from the furnace, is disposed of in as environmentally friendly a way as possible.

Example of processing a metal sulphide ore

Most lead is recovered from lead sulphide ore.

Lead ore is concentrated by crushing it to a fine powder and then separated from rock with little lead by froth flotation (see page 53). It is then roasted to convert it into lead oxide. The lead oxide is smelted with a supply of coke and limestone in a furnace. The result is not pure lead but contains small amounts of other metals.

Ingots of lead are melted and then allowed to cool. Copper has a higher melting point than lead, so as the mixture cools, crystals of copper float to the surface and can be skimmed off.

The lead is then reheated and a blast of air shot through it. This oxidises elements such as arsenic, and the oxides form a slag that can be skimmed off.

Silver and gold impurities are more soluble than lead in zinc. When zinc is added to the silver and gold they alloy with the zinc. Zinc alloy is less dense that lead, so it rises to the surface and can be skimmed off. In this way zinc, silver and gold are all removed.

The remaining material, which is already nearly pure lead, can be further refined by an electrical process called electrolysis. As a current flows through the molten lead, lead ions are attracted to the cathode of the cell and electroplated on it. When the cathode has accumulated sufficient lead, it is removed and replaced.

The vapour is then collected. Thus, for example, when zinc is smelted, the zinc vaporises and is condensed. Almost all of the impurities are removed in this way.

Refining

The final processing of an ore produces almost pure metal. This is called refining. For example, iron (in which there is about 94% iron and 6% combined impurities such as carbon, manganese, and silicon) can be refined in a vessel called a basic oxygen furnace into steel, which is iron with as little as 1% combined impurities. This is achieved with a blast of hot oxygen.

Other methods include electrolysis. If an electric current is passed through the molten material, pure metal will be deposited on one electrode. If pure lead or zinc is needed, for example, the smelted metal is refined electrically. Refining also releases gold, silver and other impurities, whose value helps to offset the extra cost of refining by electricity.

(Below) Schematic diagram of the stages in the Parke's process.

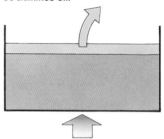

1. Impure lead ingot is melted and allowed to cool until the copper can be skimmed off.

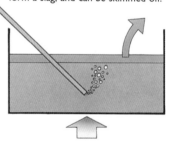

2. The lead is reheated and air blown through it. More impurities oxidise, form a slag, and can be skimmed off.

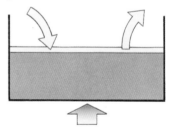

3. Some zinc is added, and the alloy that forms contains zinc, silver and gold. This is skimmed off.

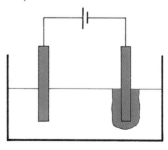

4. The lead is finally purified by making it the anode of an electrolysis cell; pure lead collects at the cathode.

Alternatively, the roasted material can be dissolved in an acid or other substance and the metal drawn off from the liquid. Oxides and sulphates are commonly refined by solution.

Refining petroleum

Natural gas is rarely processed, and is mainly used as a gas for heating purposes. Crude oil, however, is a complex mixture of chemicals that is almost unusable in its natural form and has to be processed. As there are no waste materials, as for example is the case when metal is extracted from its ore, it is simply a process of separating the chemicals (which are known as FRACTIONS). This separation stage is called refining.

One of the special properties of hydrocarbons is that any one product can be converted into any of the others. Some of the fractions are, however, less valuable than others, so a refinery must not only separate out the fractions, but convert the less desirable ones into those with a higher value.

(*Above*) The tall, slim, towers are the fractionating towers of a petrochemical plant. The squat tower on the left is the cooling tower of a power station.

The main process in a refinery is DISTILLATION. This process is done in tall towers. The crude oil is heated and fed into the lower part of the tower. The lightest fractions boil off and, as they rise through the tower, they cool and condense onto a number of specially placed shelves. The condensed liquids are then taken away. The lightest fractions include motor and aircraft fuels, and the raw materials for making carbon-based chemicals like plastics.

The products that do not boil off are collected and sent to be broken down into smaller molecules. This process is called CRACKING and it happens in another tower. The cracked fractions are then sent back for refining.

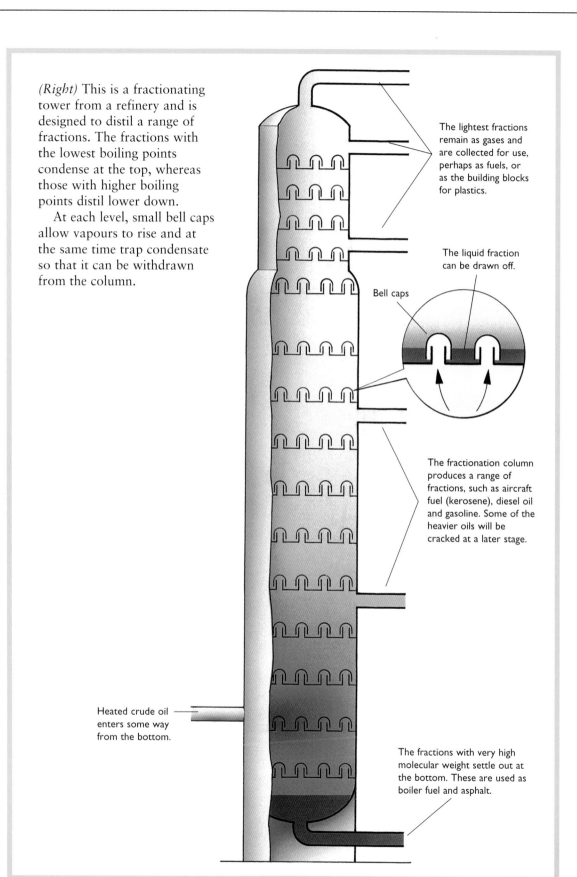

(Right) This is a fractionating tower from a refinery and is designed to distil a range of fractions. The fractions with the lowest boiling points condense at the top, whereas those with higher boiling points distil lower down.

At each level, small bell caps allow vapours to rise and at the same time trap condensate so that it can be withdrawn from the column.

The lightest fractions remain as gases and are collected for use, perhaps as fuels, or as the building blocks for plastics.

The liquid fraction can be drawn off.

Bell caps

The fractionation column produces a range of fractions, such as aircraft fuel (kerosene), diesel oil and gasoline. Some of the heavier oils will be cracked at a later stage.

Heated crude oil enters some way from the bottom.

The fractions with very high molecular weight settle out at the bottom. These are used as boiler fuel and asphalt.

Glossary

aa lava: a type of lava with a broken, bouldery surface.

abrasion: the rubbing away (erosion) of a rock by the physical scraping of particles carried by water, wind or ice.

acidic rock: a type of igneous rock that consists predominantly of light-coloured minerals and more than two-thirds silica (e.g. granite).

active volcano: a volcano that has observable signs of activity, for example, periodic plumes of steam.

adit: a horizontal tunnel drilled into rock.

aftershock: an earthquake that follows the main shock. Major earthquakes are followed by a number of aftershocks that decrease in frequency with time.

agglomerate: a rock made from the compacted particles thrown out by a volcano (e.g. tuff).

alkaline rock: a type of igneous rock containing less than half silica and normally dominated by dark-coloured minerals (e.g. gabbro).

amygdule: a vesicle in a volcanic rock filled with secondary minerals such as calcite, quartz or zeolite.

andesite: an igneous volcanic rock. Slightly more acidic than basalt.

anticline: an arching fold of rock layers in which the rocks slope down from the crest. *See also* syncline.

Appalachian Mountain (Orogenic) Belt: an old mountain range that extends for more than 3000 km along the eastern margin of North America from Alabama in the southern United States to Newfoundland, Canada, in the north. There were three Appalachian orogenies: Taconic (about 460 million years ago) in the Ordovician; Acadian (390 to 370 million years ago) in the Devonian; and Alleghenian (300 to 250 million years ago) in the Late Carboniferous to Permian. These mountain belts can be traced as the Caledonian and Hercynian orogenic belts in Europe.

Archean Eon: *see* eon.

arenaceous: a rock composed largely of sand grains.

argillaceous: a rock composed largely of clay.

arkose: a coarse sandstone formed by the disintegration of a granite.

ash, volcanic: fine powdery material thrown out of a volcano.

asthenosphere: the weak part of the upper mantle below the lithosphere, in which slow convection is thought to take place.

augite: a dark green-coloured silicate mineral containing calcium, sodium, iron, aluminium and magnesium.

axis of symmetry: a line or plane around which one part of a crystal is a mirror image of another part.

basalt: basic fine-grained igneous volcanic rock; lava often contains vesicles.

basic rock: an igneous rock (e.g. gabbro) with silica content less than two-thirds and containing a high percentage of dark-coloured minerals.

basin: a large, circular, or oval sunken region on the earth's surface created by downwards folding. A river basin, or watershed, is the area drained by a river and its tributaries.

batholith: a very large body of plutonic rock that was intruded deep into the earth's crust and is now exposed by erosion.

bauxite: a surface material that contains a high percentage of aluminium silicate. The principal ore of aluminium.

bed: a layer of sediment. It may involve many phases of deposition, each marked by a bedding plane.

bedding plane: an ancient surface on which sediment built up. Sedimentary rocks often split along bedding planes.

biotite: a black-coloured form of mica.

body wave: a seismic wave that can travel through the interior of the earth. P waves and S waves are body waves.

boss: an upwards extension of a batholith. A boss may once have been a magma chamber.

botryoidal: the shape of a mineral that resembles a bunch of grapes, e.g. haematite the crystals of which are often arranged in massive clumps, giving a surface covered with spherical bulges.

butte: a small mesa.

calcareous: composed mainly of calcium carbonate.

calcite: a mineral composed of calcium carbonate.

caldera: the collapsed cone of a volcano. It sometimes contains a crater lake.

Caledonian Mountain-Building Period, Caledonian Orogeny: a major mountain-building period in the Lower Paleozoic Era that reached its climax at the end of the Silurian Period (430 to 395 million years ago). An early phase affected only North America and made part of the Appalachian Mountain Belt.

Cambrian, Cambrian Period: the first period of geological time in the Paleozoic Era, beginning 570 million years ago and ending 500 million years ago.

carbonate minerals: minerals formed with carbonate ions (e.g. calcite).

Carboniferous, Carboniferous Period: a period of geological time between about 345 and 280 million years ago. It is often divided into the Early Carboniferous Epoch (345 to 320 million years ago) and the Late Carboniferous Epoch (320 to 280 million years ago). The Late Carboniferous is characterised by large coal-forming swamps. In North America the Carboniferous is usually divided into the Mississippian (= Lower Carboniferous) and Pennsylvanian (= Upper Carboniferous) periods.

cast, fossil: the natural filling of a mould by sediment or minerals that were left when a fossil dissolved after being enclosed by rock.

Cenozoic, Cenozoic Era: the most recent era of geological time, beginning 65 million years ago and continuing to the present.

central vent volcano: *see* stratovolcano.

chemical compound: a substance made from the chemical combination of two or more elements.

chemical rock: a rock produced by chemical precipitation (e.g. halite).

chemical weathering: the decay of a rock through the chemical action of water containing dissolved acidic gases.

cinder cone: a volcanic cone made entirely of cinders. Cinder cones have very steep sides.

class: the level of biological classification below a phylum.

clast: an individual grain of a rock.

clastic rock: a sedimentary rock that is made up of fragments of pre-existing rocks, carried by gravity, water, or wind (e.g. conglomerate, sandstone).

cleavage: the tendency of some minerals to break along one or more smooth surfaces.

coal: the carbon-rich, solid mineral derived from fossilised plant remains. Found in sedimentary rocks. Types of coal include bituminous, brown, lignite, and anthracite. A fossil fuel.

complex volcano: a volcano that has had an eruptive history and which produces two or more vents.

composite volcano: *see* stratovolcano.

concordant coast: a coast where the geological structure is parallel to the coastline. *See also* discordant coastline.

conduction (of heat): the transfer of heat between touching objects.

conglomerate: a coarse-grained sedimentary rock with grains larger than 2 mm.

contact metamorphism: metamorphism that occurs owing to direct contact with a molten magma. *See also* regional metamorphism.

continental drift: the theory suggested by Alfred Wegener that earth's continents were originally one land mass which split up to form the arrangement of continents we see today.

continental shelf: the ocean floor from the coastal shore of continents to the continental slope.

continental shield: the ancient and stable core of a tectonic plate. Also called a shield.

convection: the slow overturning of a liquid or gas that is heated from below.

cordillera: a long mountain belt consisting of many mountain ranges.

core: the innermost part of the earth. The earth's core is very dense, rich in iron, partly molten, and the source of the earth's magnetic field. The inner core is solid and has a radius of about 1300 kilometres. The outer core is fluid and is about 2100 kilometres thick. S waves cannot travel through the outer core.

cracking: the breaking up of a hydrocarbon compound into simpler constituents by means of heat.

crater lake: a lake found inside a caldera.

craton: *see* shield.

Cretaceous, Cretaceous Period: the third period of the Mesozoic Era. It lasted from about 135 to 65 million years ago. It was a time of chalk formation and when many dinosaurs lived.

cross-bedding: a pattern of deposits in a sedimentary rock in which many thin layers lie at an angle to the bedding planes, showing that the sediment was deposited by a moving fluid. Wind-deposited cross-beds are often bigger than water-deposited beds.

crust: the outermost layer of the earth, typically 5 km under the oceans and 50 to 100 km thick under continents. It makes up less than 1 per cent of the earth's volume.

crustal plate: *see* tectonic plate.

crystal: a mineral that has a regular geometric shape and is bounded by smooth, flat faces.

crystal system: a group of crystals with the same arrangement of axes.

crystalline: a mineral that has solidified but has been unable to produce well-formed crystals. Quartz and halite are commonly found as crystalline masses.

crystallisation: the formation of crystals.

cubic: a crystal system in which crystals have 3 axes all at right angles to one another and of equal length.

cuesta: a ridge in the landscape formed by a resistant band of dipping rock. A cuesta has a steep scarp slope and a more gentle dip slope.

current bedding: a pattern of deposits in a sedimentary rock in which many thin layers lie at an angle to the bedding planes, showing that the sediment was deposited by a current of water.

cyclothem: a repeating sequence of rocks found in coal strata.

delta: a triangle of deposition produced where a river enters a sea or lake.

deposit, deposition: the process of laying down material that has been transported in suspension or solution by water, ice, or wind. A deposit is the material laid down by deposition (e.g. salt deposits).

destructive plate boundary: a line where plates collide and where one plate is subducted into the mantle.

Devonian, Devonian Period: the fourth period of geological time in the Palaeozoic Era, from 395 to 345 million years ago.

diorite: an igneous plutonic rock between gabbro and granite; the plutonic equivalent of andesite.

dip: the angle that a bedding plane or fault makes with the horizontal.

dip slope: the more gently sloping part of a cuesta whose surface often parallels the dip of the strata.

discontinuity: a gap in deposition, perhaps caused by the area being lifted above the sea so that erosion, rather than deposition, occurred for a time.

discordant coast: a coast where the rock structure is at an angle to the line of the coast. *See also* concordant coastline.

displacement: the distance over which one piece of rock is pushed relative to another.

dissolve: to break down a substance into a solution without causing a reaction.

distillation: the boiling off of volatile materials, leaving a residue.

dolomite: a mineral composed of calcium magnesium carbonate.

dome: a circular, uplifted region of rocks taking the shape of a dome and found in some areas of folded rocks. Rising plugs of salt will also dome up the rocks above them. They sometimes make oil traps.

dormant volcano: a volcano that shows no signs of activity but which has been active in the recent past.

drift: a tunnel drilled in rock and designed to provide a sloping route for carrying out ore or coal by means of a conveyor belt.

dyke: a wall-like sheet of igneous rock that cuts across the layers of the surrounding rocks.

dyke swarm: a collection of hundreds or thousands of parallel dykes.

earthquake: shaking of the earth's surface caused by a sudden movement of rock within the earth.

element: a fundamental chemical building block. A substance that cannot be separated into simpler substances by any chemical means. Oxygen and sulphur are examples of elements.

eon: the largest division of geological time. An eon is subdivided into eras. Precambrian time is divided into the Archean (earlier than 2.5 billion years ago) and Proterozoic eons (more recent than 2.5 billion years ago). The Phanerozoic Eon includes the Cambrian Period to the present.

epicentre: the point on the earth's surface directly above the focus (hypocentre) of an earthquake.

epoch: a subdivision of a geological period in the geological time scale (e.g. Pleistocene Epoch).

era: a subdivision of a geological eon in the geological time scale (e.g. Cenozoic Era). An era is subdivided into periods.

erode, erosion: the twin processes of breaking down a rock (called weathering) and then removing the debris (called transporting).

escarpment: the crest of a ridge made of dipping rocks.

essential mineral: the dominant mineral constituents of a rock used to classify it.

evaporite: a mineral or rock formed as the result of evaporation of salt-laden water, such as a lagoon or salt lake.

exoskeleton: another word for shell. Applies to invertebrates.

extinct volcano: a volcano that has shown no signs of activity in historic times.

extrusive rock, extrusion: an igneous volcanic rock that has solidified on the surface of the earth.

facet: the cleaved face of a mineral. Used in describing jewellery.

facies: physical, chemical, or biological variations in a sedimentary bed of the same geological age (e.g. sandy facies, limestone facies).

family: a part of the classification of living things above a genus.

fault: a deep fracture or zone of fractures in rocks along which there has been displacement of one side relative to the other. It represents a weak point in the crust and upper mantle.

fault scarp: a long, straight, steep slope in the landscape that has been produced by faulting.

feldspar: the most common silicate mineral. It consists of two forms: plagioclase and orthoclase.

ferromagnesian mineral: dark-coloured minerals, such as augite and hornblende, which contain relatively high proportions of iron and magnesium and low proportions of silica.

fissure: a substantial crack in a rock.

fjord: a glaciated valley in a mountainous area coastal area that has been partly flooded by the sea.

focal depth: the depth of an earthquake focus below the surface.

focus: the origin of an earthquake, directly below the epicentre.

fold: arched or curved rock strata.

fold axis: line following the highest arching in an anticline, or the lowest arching in a syncline.

fold belt: a part of a mountain system containing folded sedimentary rocks.

foliation: a texture of a rock (usually schist) that resembles the pages in a book.

formation: a word used to describe a collection of related rock layers or beds. A number of related beds make a member; a collection of related members makes up a formation. Formations are often given location names, e.g. Toroweap Formation, the members of which are a collection of dominantly limestone beds.

fossil: any evidence of past life, including remains, traces and imprints.

fossil fuel: any fuel that was formed in the geological past from the remains of living organisms. The main fossil fuels are coal and petroleum (oil and natural gas).

fraction: one of the components of crude oil that can be separated from others by heating and then by cooling the vapour.

fracture: a substantial break across a rock.

fracture zone: a region in which fractures are common. Fracture zones are particularly common in folded rock and near faults.

frost shattering: the process of breaking pieces of rock through the action of freezing and melting of rainwater

gabbro: alkaline igneous plutonic rock, typically showing dark-coloured crystals; plutonic equivalent of basalt.

gallery: a horizontal access tunnel in a mine.

gangue: the unwanted mineral matter found in association with a metal.

gem: a mineral, usually in crystal form, that is regarded as having particular beauty and value.

genus: (*pl.* genera) the biological classification for a group of closely related species.

geode: a hollow lump of rock (nodule) that often contains crystals.

geological column: a columnar diagram showing the divisions of geological time (eons, eras, periods, and epochs).

geological eon: *see* eon.

geological epoch: *see* epoch.

geological era: *see* era.

geological period: a subdivision of a geological era (e.g. Carboniferous Period). A period is subdivided into epochs.

geological system: a term for an accumulation of strata that occurs during a geological period (e.g. the Ordovician System is the rocks deposited during the Ordovician Period). Systems are divided into series.

geological time: the history of the earth revealed by its rocks.

geological time scale: the division of geological time into eons, era, periods, and epochs.

geosyncline: a large, slowly subsiding region marginal to a continent where huge amounts of sediment accumulate. The rocks in a geosyncline are eventually lifted to form mountain belts.

gneiss: a metamorphic rock showing large grains.

graben: a fallen block of the earth's crust forming a long trough, separated on all sides by faults. Associated with rift valleys.

grain: a particle of a rock or mineral.

granite: an acidic, igneous, plutonic rock containing free quartz, typically light in colour; plutonic equivalent of rhyolite.

grit: grains larger than sand but smaller than stones.

groundmass: *see* matrix.

group: a word used to describe a collection of related rock layers, or beds. A number of related beds make a member; a collection of related members makes up a formation; a collection of related formations makes a group.

gypsum: a mineral made of calcium sulphate.

halide minerals: a group of minerals (e.g. halite) that contain a halogen element (elements similar to chlorine) bonded with another element. Many are evaporite minerals.

halite: a mineral made of sodium chloride.

Hawaiian-type eruption: a name for a volcanic eruption that mainly consists of lava fountains.

hexagonal: a crystal system in which crystals have 3 axes all at 120 degrees to one another and of equal length.

hogback: a cuesta where the scarp and dip slopes are at about the same angle.

hornblende: a dark-green silicate mineral of the amphibole group containing sodium, potassium, calcium, magnesium, iron and aluminium.

horst: a raised block of the earth's crust separated on all sides by faults. Associated with rift valleys.

hot spot: a place where a fixed mantle magma plume reaches the surface.

hydraulic action: the erosive action of water pressure on rocks.

hydrothermal: a change brought about in a rock or mineral due to the action of superheated mineral-rich fluids, usually water.

hypocentre: the calculated location of the focus of an earthquake.

ice wedging: *see* frost shattering.

Icelandic-type eruption: a name given to a fissure type of eruption.

igneous rock: rock formed by the solidification of magma. Igneous rocks include volcanic and plutonic rocks.

impermeable: a rock that will not allow a liquid to pass through it.

imprint: a cast left by a former life form.

impurities: small amounts of elements or compounds in an otherwise homogeneous mineral.

index fossil: a fossil used as a marker for a particular part of geological time.

intrusive rock, intrusion: rocks that have formed from cooling magma below the surface. When inserted amongst other rocks, intruded rocks are called an intrusion.

invertebrate: an animal with an external skeleton.

ion: a charged particle.

island arc: a pattern of volcanic islands that follows the shape of an arc when seen from above.

isostacy: the principle that a body can float in a more dense fluid. The same as buoyancy, but used for continents.

joint: a significant crack between blocks of rock, normally used in the context of patterns of cracks.

Jurassic, Jurassic Period: the second geological period in the Mesozoic Era, lasting from about 190 to 135 million years ago.

kingdom: the broadest division in the biological classification of living things.

laccolith: a lens-shaped body of intrusive igneous rock with a dome-shaped upper surface and a flat bottom surface.

landform: a recognisable shape of part of the landscape, for example, a cuesta.

landslide: the rapid movement of a slab of soil down a steep hillslope.

lateral fault: *see* thrust fault.

laterite: a surface deposit containing a high proportion of iron.

lava: molten rock material extruded onto the surface of the earth.

lava bomb: *see* volcanic bomb.

law of superposition: the principle that younger rock is deposited on older.

limestone: a carbonate sedimentary rock composed of more than half calcium carbonate.

lithosphere: that part of the crust and upper mantle which is brittle and makes up the tectonic plates.

lode: a mining term for a rock containing many rich ore-bearing minerals. Similar to vein.

Love wave, L wave: a major type of surface earthquake wave that shakes the ground surface at right angles to the direction in which the wave is travelling. It is named after A.E.H. Love, the English mathematician who discovered it.

lustre: the way in which a mineral reflects light. Used as a test when identifying minerals.

magma: the molten material that comes from the mantle and which cools to form igneous rocks.

magma chamber: a large cavity melted in the earth's crust and filled with magma. Many magma chambers are plumes of magma that have melted their way from the mantle to the upper part of the crust. When a magma chamber is no longer supplied with molten magma, the magma solidifies to form a granite batholith.

mantle: the layer of the earth between the crust and the core. It is approximately 2900 kilometres thick and is the largest of the earth's major layers.

marginal accretion: the growth of mountain belts on the edges of a shield.

mass extinction: a time when the majority of species on the planet were killed off.

matrix: the rock or sediment in which a fossil is embedded; the fine-grained rock in which larger particles are embedded, for example, in a conglomerate.

mechanical weathering: the disintegration of a rock by frost shattering/ice wedging.

mesa: a large detached piece of a tableland.

Mesozoic, Mesozoic Era: the geological era between the Palaeozoic and the Cenozoic eras. It lasted from about 225 to 65 million years ago.

metamorphic aureole: the region of contact metamorphic rock that surrounds a batholith.

metamorphic rock: any rock (e.g. schist, gneiss) that was formed from a pre-existing rock by heat and pressure.

meteorite: a substantial chunk of rock in space.

micas: a group of soft, sheet-like silicate minerals (e.g. biotite, muscovite).

mid-ocean ridge: a long mountain chain on the ocean floor where basalt periodically erupts, forming new oceanic crust.

mineral: a naturally occurring inorganic substance of definite chemical composition (e.g. calcite, calcium carbonate).

More generally, any resource extracted from the ground by mining (includes metal ores, coal, oil, gas, rocks, etc.).

mineral environment: the place where a mineral or a group of associated minerals form. Mineral environments include igneous, sedimentary, and metamorphic rocks.

mineralisation: the formation of minerals within a rock.

Modified Mercalli Scale: a scale for measuring the impact of an earthquake. It is composed of 12 increasing levels of intensity, which range from imperceptible, designated by Roman numeral I, to catastrophic destruction, designated by XII.

Mohorovicic discontinuity: the boundary surface that separates the earth's crust from the underlying mantle. Named after Andrija Mohorovicic, a Croatian seismologist.

Mohs' Scale of Hardness: a relative scale developed to put minerals into an order. The hardest is 10 (diamond), and the softest is 1 (talc).

monoclinic: a crystal system in which crystals have 2 axes all at right angles to one another, and each axis is of unequal length.

mould: an impression in a rock of the outside of an organism.

mountain belt: a region where there are many ranges of mountains. The term is often applied to a wide belt of mountains produced during mountain building.

mountain building: the creation of mountains as a result of the collision of tectonic plates. Long belts or chains of mountains can form along the edge of a continent during this process. Mountain building is also called orogeny.

mountain building period: a period during which a geosyncline is compressed into fold mountains by the collision of two tectonic plates. Also known as orogenesis.

mudstone: a fine-grained, massive rock formed by the compaction of mud.

nappe: a piece of a fold that has become detached from its roots during intensive mountain building.

native metal: a metal that occurs uncombined with any other element.

natural gas: *see* petroleum.

normal fault: a fault in which one block has slipped down the face of another. It is the most common kind of fault and results from tension.

nuée ardente: another word for pyroclastic flow.

ocean trench: a deep, steep-sided trough in the ocean floor caused by the subduction of oceanic crust beneath either other oceanic crust or continental crust.

olivine: the name of a group of magnesium iron silicate minerals that have an olive colour.

order: a level of biological classification between class and family.

Ordovician, Ordovician Period: the second period of geological time within the Palaeozoic Era. It lasted from about 500 to 430 million years ago.

ore: a rock containing enough useful metal or fuel to be worth mining.

ore mineral: a mineral that occurs in sufficient quantity to be mined for its metal. The compound must also be easy to process.

organic rocks: rocks formed by living things, for example, coal.

orthoclase: the form of feldspar that is often pink in colour and which contains potassium as important ions.

orogenic belt: a mountain belt.

orogeny: a period of mountain building. Orogenesis is the process of mountain building and the creation of orogenic belts.

orthorhombic: a crystal system in which crystals have 3 axes all at right angles to one another but of unequal length.

outcrop: the exposure of a rock at the surface of the earth.

overburden: the unwanted layer(s) of rock above an ore or coal body.

oxide minerals: a group of minerals in which oxygen is a major constituent. A compound in which oxygen is bonded to another element or group.

Pacific Ring of Fire: the ring of volcanoes and volcanic activity that circles the Pacific Ocean. Created by the collision of the Pacific Plate with its neighbouring plates.

pahoehoe lava: the name for a form of lava that has a smooth surface.

Palaeozoic, Palaeozoic Era: a major interval of geological time. The Palaeozoic is the oldest era in which fossil life is commonly found. It lasted from about 570 to 225 million years ago.

palaeomagnetism: the natural magnetic traces that reveal the intensity and direction of the earth's magnetic field in the geological past.

pegmatite: an igneous rock (e.g. a dyke) of extremely coarse crystals.

Pelean-type eruption: a violent explosion dominated by pyroclastic flows.

period: *see* geological period.

permeable rock: a rock that will allow a fluid to pass through it.

Permian, Permian Period: the last period of the Palaeozoic Era, lasting from about 280 to 225 million years ago.

petrified: when the tissues of a dead plant or animal have been replaced by minerals, such as silica, they are said to be petrified (e.g. petrified wood).

petrified forest: a large number of fossil trees. Most petrified trees are replaced by silica.

petroleum: the carbon-rich, and mostly liquid, mixture produced by the burial and partial alteration of animal and plant remains. Petroleum is found in many sedimentary rocks. The liquid part of petroleum is called oil, the gaseous part is known as natural gas. Petroleum is an important fossil fuel.

petroleum field: a region from which petroleum can be recovered.

Phanerozoic Eon: the most recent eon, beginning at the Cambrian Period, some 570 million years ago, and extending up to the present.

phenocryst: an especially large crystal (in a porphyritic rock), embedded in smaller mineral grains.

phylum: (*pl.* phyla) biological classification for one of the major divisions of animal life and second in complexity to kingdom. The plant kingdom is not divided into phyla but into divisions.

placer deposit: a sediment containing heavy metal grains (e.g. gold) that have weathered out of the bedrock and are concentrated on a stream bed or along a coast.

plagioclase: the form of feldspar that is often white or grey and which contains sodium and calcium as important ions.

planetismals: small embryo planets.

plate: *see* tectonic plate.

plateau: an extensive area of raised flat land. The cliff-like edges of a plateau may, when eroded, leave isolated features such as mesas and buttes. *See also* tableland.

plate tectonics: the theory that the earth's crust and upper mantle (the lithosphere) are broken into a number of more or less rigid, but constantly moving, slabs or plates.

Plinian-type eruption: an explosive eruption that sends a column of ash high into the air.

plug: *see* volcanic plug

plunging fold: a fold whose axis dips, or plunges, into the ground.

plutonic rock: an igneous rock that has solidified at great depth and contains large crystals due to the slowness of cooling (e.g. granite, gabbro).

porphyry, porphyritic rock: an igneous rock in which larger crystals (phenocrysts) are enclosed in a fine-grained matrix.

Precambrian, Precambrian time: the whole of earth history before the Cambrian Period. Also called Precambrian Era and Precambrian Eon.

precipitate: a substance that has settled out of a liquid as a result of a chemical reaction between two chemicals in the liquid.

Primary Era: an older name for the Palaeozoic Era.

prismatic: a word used to describe a mineral that has formed with one axis very much longer than the others.

Proterozoic Eon: *see* eon.

P wave, primary wave, primary seismic wave: P waves are the fastest body waves. The waves carry energy in the same line as the direction of the wave. P waves can travel through all layers of the earth and are generally felt as a thump. *See also* S wave.

pyrite: iron sulphide. It is common in sedimentary rocks that were poor in oxygen, and sometimes forms fossil casts.

pyroclastic flow: solid material ejected from a volcano, combined with searingly hot gases, which together behave as a high-density fluid. Pyroclastic flows can do immense damage, as was the case with Mount Saint Helens.

pyroclastic material: any solid material ejected from a volcano.

Quaternary, Quaternary Period: the second period in the Cenozoic Era, beginning about 1.6 million years ago and continuing to the present day.

radiation: the transfer of energy between objects that are not in contact.

radioactive dating: the dating of a material by the use of its radioactive elements. The rate of decay of any element changes in a predictable way, allowing a precise date to be given of when the material was formed.

rank: a name used to describe the grade of coal in terms of its possible heat output. The higher the rank, the more the heat output.

Rayleigh wave: a type of surface wave having an elliptical motion similar to the waves caused when a stone is dropped into a pond. It is the slowest, but often the largest and most destructive, of the wave types caused by an earthquake. It is usually felt as a rolling or rocking motion and, in the case of major earthquakes, can be seen as they approach. Named after Lord Rayleigh, the English physicist who predicted its existence.

regional metamorphism: metamorphism resulting from both heat and pressure. It is usually connected with mountain building and occurs over a large area. *See also* contact metamorphism.

reniform: a kidney-shaped mineral habit (e.g. hematite).

reservoir rock: a permeable rock in which petroleum accumulates.

reversed fault: a fault where one slab of the earth's crust rides up over another. Reversed faults are only common during plate collision.

rhyolite: acid, igneous, volcanic rock, typically light in colour; volcanic equivalent of granite.

ria: the name for a partly flooded coastal river valley in an area where the landscape is hilly.

Richter Scale: the system used to measure the strength of an earthquake. Developed by Charles Richter, an American, in 1935.

rift, rift valley: long troughs on continents and mid-ocean ridges that are bounded by normal faults.

rifting: the process of crustal stretching that causes blocks of crust to subside, creating rift valleys.

rock: a naturally occurring solid material containing one or more minerals.

rock cycle: the continuous sequence of events that cause mountains to be formed, then eroded, before being formed again.

rupture: the place over which an earthquake causes rocks to move against one another.

salt dome: a balloon-shaped mass of salt produced by salt being forced upwards under pressure.

sandstone: a sedimentary rock composed of cemented sand-sized grains 0.06–2 mm in diameter.

scarp slope: the steep slope of a cuesta.

schist: a metamorphic rock characterised by a shiny surface of mica crystals all orientated in the same direction.

scoria: the rough, often foam-like rock that forms on the surface of some lavas.

seamount: a volcano that rises from the sea bed.

Secondary Era: an older term for a geological era. Now replaced by Mesozoic Era.

sediment: any solid material that has settled out of suspension in a liquid.

sedimentary rock: a layered clastic rock formed through the deposition of pieces of mineral, rock, animal or vegetable matter.

segregation: the separation of minerals.

seismic gap: a part of an active fault where there have been no earthquakes in recent times.

seismic wave: a wave generated by an earthquake.

series: the rock layers that correspond to an epoch of time.

shadow zone: the region of the earth that experiences no shocks after an earthquake.

shaft: a vertical tunnel that provides access or ventilation to a mine.

shale: a fine-grained sedimentary rock made of clay minerals with particle sizes smaller than 2 microns.

shield: the ancient and stable core of a tectonic plate. Also called a continental shield.

shield volcano: a volcano with a broad, low-angled cone made entirely of lava.

silica, silicate: silica is silicon dioxide. It is a very common mineral, occurring as quartz, chalcedony, etc. A silicate is any mineral that contains silica.

sill: a tabular, sheet-like body of intrusive igneous rock that has been injected between layers of sedimentary or metamorphic rock.

Silurian, Silurian Period: the name of the third geological period of the Palaeozoic Era. It began about 430 and ended about 395 million years ago.

skarn: a mineral deposit formed by the chemical reaction of hot acidic fluids and carbonate rocks.

slag: waste rock material that becomes separated from the metal during smelting.

slate: a low-grade metamorphic rock produced by pressure, in which the clay minerals have arranged themselves parallel to one another.

slaty cleavage: a characteristic pattern found in slates in which the parallel arrangement of clay minerals causes the rock to fracture (cleave) in sheets.

species: a population of animals or plants capable of interbreeding.

spreading boundary: a line where two plates are being pulled away from each other. New crust is formed as molten rock is forced upwards into the gap.

stock: a vertical protrusion of a batholith that pushes up closer to the surface.

stratigraphy: the study of the earth's rocks in the context of their history and conditions of formation.

stratovolcano: a tall volcanic mountain made of alternating layers, or strata, of ash and lava.

stratum: (*pl.* strata) a layer of sedimentary rock.

streak: the colour of the powder of a mineral produced by rubbing the mineral against a piece of unglazed, white porcelain. Used as a test when identifying minerals.

striation: minute parallel grooves on crystal faces.

strike, direction of: the direction of a bedding plane or fault at right angles to the dip.

Strombolian-type eruption: a kind of volcanic eruption that is explosive enough to send out some volcanic bombs.

subduction: the process of one tectonic plate descending beneath another.

subduction zone: the part of the earth's surface along which one tectonic plate descends into the mantle. It is often shaped in the form of an number of arcs.

sulphides: a group of important ore minerals (e.g. pyrite, galena, and sphalerite) in which sulphur combines with one or more metals.

surface wave: any one of a number of waves such as Love waves or Rayleigh waves that shake the ground surface just after an earthquake. *See also* Love waves and Rayleigh waves.

suture: the junction of 2 or more parts of a skeleton; in cephalopods the junction of a septum with the inner surface of the shell wall. It is very distinctive in ammonoids and used to identify them.

S wave, shear or secondary seismic wave: this kind of wave carries energy through the earth like a rope being shaken. S waves cannot travel through the outer core of the earth because they cannot pass through fluids. *See also* P wave.

syncline: a downfold of rock layers in which the rocks slope up from the bottom of the fold. *See also* anticline.

system: see geological system.

tableland: another word for a plateau. *See* plateau.

tectonic plate: one of the great slabs, or plates, of the lithosphere (the earth's crust and part of the earth's upper mantle) that covers the whole of the earth's surface. The earth's plates are separated by zones of volcanic and earthquake activity.

Tertiary, Tertiary Period: the first period of the Cenozoic Era. It began 665 and ended about 1.6 million years ago.

thrust fault: *see* reversed fault.

transcurrent fault: *see* lateral fault.

transform fault: *see* lateral fault.

translucent: a description of a mineral that allows light to penetrate but not pass through.

transparent: a description of a mineral that allows light to pass right through.

trellis drainage pattern: a river drainage system where the trunk river and its tributaries tend to meet at right angles.

trench: *see* ocean trench.

Triassic, Triassic Period: the first period of the Mesozoic era. It lasted from about 225 to 190 million years ago.

triclinic: a crystal system in which crystals have 3 axes, none at right angles or of equal length to one another.

tsunami: a very large wave produced by an underwater earthquake.

tuff: a rock made from volcanic ash.

unconformity: any interruption in the depositional sequence of sedimentary rocks.

valve: in bivalves and brachiopods, one of the separate parts of the shell.

vein: a sheet-like body of mineral matter (e.g. quartz) that cuts across a rock. Veins are often important sources of valuable minerals. Miners call such important veins lodes.

vent: the vertical pipe that allows the passage of magma through the centre of a volcano.

vertebrate: an animal with an internal skeleton.

vesicle: a small cavity in a volcanic rock originally created by an air bubble trapped in the molten lava.

viscous, viscosity: sticky, stickiness.

volatile: substances that tend to evaporate or boil off of a liquid.

volcanic: anything from, or of, a volcano. Volcanic rocks are igneous rocks that cool as they are released at the earth's surface – including those formed underwater; typically have small crystals due to the rapid cooling, e.g. basalt, andesite and rhyolite.

volcanic bomb: a large piece of magma thrown out of a crater during an eruption, which solidifies as it travels through cool air.

volcanic eruption: an ejection of ash or lava from a volcano.

volcanic glass: lava that has solidified very quickly and has not had time to develop any crystals. Obsidian is a volcanic glass.

volcanic plug: the solidified core of an extinct volcano.

Vulcanian-type eruption: an explosive form of eruption without a tall ash column or pyroclastic flow.

water gap: a gap cut by a superimposed river, which is still occupied by the river.

weather, weathered, weathering: the process of weathering is the mechanical action of ice and the chemical action of rainwater on rock, breaking it down into small pieces that can then be carried away. *See also* chemical weathering and mechanical weathering.

wind gap: a gap cut by a superimposed river, which is no longer occupied by the river.

Set Index